I0154945

# Henry the Tudor Dude

## A Musical Play

## Kjartan Poskitt

A SAMUEL FRENCH ACTING EDITION

# SAMUEL FRENCH

FOUNDED 1830

SAMUELFRENCH-LONDON.CO.UK
SAMUELFRENCH.COM

Copyright © 1995 by Kjartan Poskitt
All Rights Reserved

*HENRY THE TUDOR DUDE* is fully protected under the copyright laws of the British Commonwealth, including Canada, the United States of America, and all other countries of the Copyright Union. All rights, including professional and amateur stage productions, recitation, lecturing, public reading, motion picture, radio broadcasting, television and the rights of translation into foreign languages are strictly reserved.

ISBN 978-0-573-08101-9

www.samuelfrench-london.co.uk

www.samuelfrench.com

## FOR AMATEUR PRODUCTION ENQUIRIES

### UNITED  KINGDOM  AND  WORLD
### EXCLUDING NORTH AMERICA
plays@SamuelFrench-London.co.uk
### 020 7255 4302/01

Each title is subject to availability from Samuel French,

depending upon country of performance.

CAUTION: Professional and amateur producers are hereby warned that *HENRY THE TUDOR DUDE* is subject to a licensing fee. Publication of this play does not imply availability for performance. Both amateurs and professionals considering a production are strongly advised to apply to the appropriate agent before starting rehearsals, advertising, or booking a theatre. A licensing fee must be paid whether the title is presented for charity or gain and whether or not admission is charged.

The professional rights in this play are controlled by Tessa Le Bars Mangement, 54 Birchwood Rd, Orpington BR5 1NZ.

No one shall make any changes in this title for the purpose of production. No part of this book may be reproduced, stored in a retrieval system, or transmitted in any form, by any means, now known or yet to be invented, including mechanical, electronic, photocopying, recording, videotaping, or otherwise, without the prior written permission of the publisher. No one shall upload this title, or part of this title, to any social media websites.

The right of Kjartan Poskitt to be identified as author of this work has been asserted by him in accordance with Section 77 of the Copyright, Designs and Patents Act 1988

**HENRY THE TUDOR DUDE**

The first productions were by:

The Edge Hill Players, Wimbledon, London, on 22nd January, 1994;

and Staunton Park School, Havant, on 15th February, 1994.

# CHARACTERS

**News-reader**, for Tudor News
**Reporter**, for Tudor News
**Latin Correspondent**, for Tudor News
**Henry VIII**
**Peg** ⎫
**Maud** ⎬ Palace servants
**Joan** ⎭
**Empson** ⎫
**Dudley** ⎬ Henry VII's tax collectors
**Executioner**
**Boy Henry**, Henry as a boy
**Nanny**
**Will Sommers**, the jester
**Lady Adie**, the war correspondent for Tudor News
**Holbein**, the artist
**Pietro Torrigiano**, the sculptor
**The Pope Clement VII**
**Guiseppe**, the Pope's henchman
**Doctor**
**Midwife**
**Judge**
**Catherine Of Aragon** ⎫
**Anne Boleyn**
**Jane Seymour** ⎬ Henry's wives
**Anne Of Cleeves**
**Catherine Howard**
**Catherine Parr** ⎭
**Mary**, Catherine of Aragon's teenage daughter
**Charles V**, the King of Spain
**Thomas Wolsey** ⎫
**Thomas Cranmer** ⎬ Henry's aides
**Thomas More**
**Thomas Cromwell** ⎭

There are many other parts, including:

**Jurors, Mourners, Courtiers, Pages, Warders, Girls, Soldiers, Germans, Waiters, Maids...**

# Addenda to the 2001 reprint

## Cutting Suggestion : "Big Bessie"

As stated in the introduction you are more than welcome to cut the text to suit your company. In particular many companies opt to leave one or two songs out, and in most cases the narrative runs quite smoothly without them. However, if "Big Bessie" is cut, sadly the formidable Elizabeth I escapes the show with hardly a mention, so if you are thinking of leaving "Big Bessie" out it would be nice to replace it with this section:

Bottom of page 48:

**Henry** It's pathetic, isn't it? Peasants can have sons, serfs can have sons, dogs, mice and fish can have sons, but not me.

*Henry exits*

**News-reader** We now have a rather strange report that suggests Henry is quite wrong to underestimate his second daughter. For a bizarre glimpse of the future, we turn to the Court Clairvoyant.

*Joan enters*

**Joan**     Elizabeth will take the throne
The greatest Queen the world has known
For five and forty years she'll reign
And defeat the Armada sent from Spain.

*Joan exits*

**News-reader** Makes you think, doesn't it?

*Lights dim to represent a dank prison cell*

(continue on page 50)

# MUSICAL NUMBERS

## ACT I

1 **The Coronation Song**      Everybody
A soft choral introduction builds into a majestic theme to mark the coronation.

2 **The Body Rock**      Crowd, Empson and Dudley
The Body Rock is the theme to the show. It's a very solid rock number, ideal for the crowd to chant away to as Henry's victims are despatched!

3 **I Wanna Be Queen!**      Court Girls
A gentle vaudeville number for the disappointed "wannabes".

4 **The Battle Of The Spurs**      Henry and Soldiers
A song with a solid beaty chorus for all the jeering English soldiers.

5 **Wonderful Waste Of Time**      Wolsey and Everybody
A dapper little number to announce the most fabulous party ever held.

6 **Six Finger Annie**      Courtiers
Fast and serious rock featuring "glitter" backing vocals and a wicked electric lute solo!

7 **Do Your Worst**      Catherine of Aragon, Mary and ladies in waiting
A bitter yet melodious song about Henry's behaviour.

8 **The Three Toms**      Cromwell, More and Cranmer and Courtiers
Slick words to a modern dance beat.
**The Body Rock Instrumental**
To round off Act I.

## ACT II

The musical score is available on sale from Samuel French Ltd

A cassette of the music is available on free loan so you may hear the music before committing yourself to a production.

In some instances, the music on the tape may be set in a different key to that shown on the Vocal Score.
Some of the backing tracks have had their introductions lengthened or otherwise altered to make them more convenient to use in live performances.

All tracks were written and recorded by Kjartan Poskitt with additional vocals by Carol Turner.

In addition, an arrangement for a **five-piece band** is available from the author via Samuel French Ltd.

## Pronunciation guide to Spanish dialogue

**Catherine A** *'Enry! Pedazo de animal!* (Page 16)
*Pedasso de animal!*

**Catherine A** Que te as creido que eres? (Page 16)
*Kay tay as crey-ee-doh kay erris?*

**Charles** Que passa aqui? (Page 32)
*Kay passa ackee?*

**Charles** *Con mucho cuidado!* (Page 32)
*Kon musho quee-dah-doh!*
(meaning "watch it!")

## Use of additional material

As suggested in the Introduction, please feel welcome to cut any songs or dialogue to make the show more suitable for your company, and do feel free to alter <u>one or two lines</u> to make funny topical or local references. However, please DO NOT add lots of extra dialogue and DO NOT put in other songs!

Kjartan Poskitt

**Website**
Soundbites from the songs from this, and other Kjartan Poskitt shows, together with further information can be found on the author's website at:
<u>www.kjartan.co.uk</u>

# INTRODUCTION

**Why I wrote *Henry the Tudor Dude***
The first reason is that Henry was a good old thunderous character, and his story is long overdue on a stage. Although the early sixteenth century was quite a complicated piece of history, I have endeavoured to unravel it as accurately as possible and present it in a form that will entertain both the cast and the audience.

My second reason is that I wanted to create a fun show suitable for a large cast of young performers. By a large cast I mean about fifty performers, but the show could be performed by any number between ten and infinity. By young performers I had intended that the show should be suitable for a cast aged between eight and eighteen; however, I've been delighted to find that I had underestimated Henry's universal appeal!

**Historical accuracy**
All the facts and dates are correct, but sadly it has not been possible to cover absolutely everything. Henry's relationship with Parliament, his building of the Navy and Cinque Ports, and a lot of the European history have largely had to be ignored. The only liberty I've taken is in some of the dialogue, but I deliberately wanted to give the actors lines they could deliver easily and with fun, rather than have us all try to compete with Shakespeare.

**Cutting the text**
The complete show runs to about one hour and fifty minutes excluding the interval, but if desired, producers are most welcome to cut any unneeded songs or dialogue. Any gaps left in the story can be covered by giving the News-reader a few extra lines. (A hint: if the News-reader ends up with a great deal to do, then the part could be adapted for two News-readers. One of these could also double as the Reporter and Lady Adie if necessary.)

**Doubling parts**
To mount the complete show, all but the very largest companies will find they need to do some doubling. Happily, Henry didn't let most people live

too long, so doubling is not too complicated! Most of the smaller parts can be doubled, and some even dispensed with as necessary to suit the company. The role of Henry himself is immense; if necessary, a second actor could take over after the interval!

A good way of seeing how best to arrange the parts is to have a small company read through. Many of the major parts can be neatly combined; here's just a few examples: Wolsey and the Judge, Will Sommers and the Executioner (and possibly Guiseppe as well), Peg and Lady Adie and Anne of Cleves, Maud and Catherine Howard, Joan and Catherine Parr. The smaller parts are ideal for when people have big gaps between major scenes, otherwise they can usually be written out. The choruses to sing the songs can be made up of anyone. (If necessary, a flamboyant costume can be quickly covered with a cloak).

By cutting and doubling, I hope any company will have the best opportunity to create their own customised version of *Henry*!

## Scenery

The only permanent item of scenery is a News-reader's desk set off to one side of the stage. This should leave the main part of the stage clear so that any chairs or other items can be quickly brought on or struck as necessary. Any additional scenery is purely at the discretion of the company.

## Music

A cassette tape is available which not only has demonstrations of all the songs, but also the backing music recorded separately, should companies wish to use it. Printed music is available as a vocal score, i.e., melodies and chords with some backing/harmony suggestions.

Kjartan Poskitt

# HISTORICAL BACKGROUND

As well as being a lively musical entertainment, *Henry The Tudor Dude* accurately relates the life of King Henry VIII.

Although it was not possible to include every detail of Henry's reign, as many relevant facts as possible were included. The outline of the show is set out below.

## Early popularity

Henry is crowned in Westminster Abbey in 1509 AD at the age of eighteen. He has succeeded his late father Henry VII. He is young, fit, handsome and very popular.

Henry executes his father's notorious tax collectors Empson and Dudley. Thomas Wolsey takes over many of Henry's duties as Henry is too busy enjoying life.

Henry was betrothed to his late brother's widow Catherine of Aragon when he was ten. Within two months of his coronation he marries the Spanish Catherine.

Henry and Catherine's father Ferdinand unite to attack France, but Henry's troops get disillusioned with Ferdinand and finally mutiny.

Henry launches his own attack on northern France which results in the French fleeing at the Battle of the Spurs. Meanwhile, Wolsey suppresses an invasion from Scotland. For his efforts, Wolsey is made Chancellor and Archbishop of York.

Catherine finally gives birth to a surviving child, who is Mary. Although Henry wants a son, this first daughter does not yet cause concern.

Meanwhile, Wolsey arranges a huge pageant in France in the guise of a peace treaty. It is the fabulous Field of the Cloth of Gold which despite its grandeur was historically insignificant.

The Pope is pleased with Henry's Catholic ways and makes him *Fidei Defensor*—Defender of the Faith.

## Desperation

Catherine is approaching her fortieth birthday and still has only the one child Mary.

Henry is getting desperate for a legitimate son for the country's stability. A very attractive new girl arrives at court and Henry's eye roves towards her. She is Anne Boleyn.

## A messy divorce

Henry instructs Wolsey to ask the Pope to grant him a divorce. This was not unusual; Henry's sister had had one before. Henry also claimed that a clause in the Bible stated that his marriage to his brother's widow had never been valid.

The Pope at this time is under the influence of Charles of Spain, who is Catherine's nephew. Charles tells the Pope to refuse the divorce.

Henry sees this as a failure on Wolsey's part and starts to take on new advisors; namely, Thomas More, Thomas Cranmer, and Thomas Cromwell.

Wolsey is summoned from York but dies on the way to his trial. Henry is impatient to marry Anne.

Cranmer informs him that he should go ahead and divorce Catherine to marry Anne anyway, as many European scholars feel that Charles' influence on the Pope is wrong.

Cranmer is appointed Archbishop of Canterbury.

## The Reformation

Henry decides to break with the Roman Catholic Church, thus allowing himself a divorce from Catherine. Thomas More cannot agree with this and pressure is put on him. Thomas Cromwell on the other hand starts breaking up churches and monasteries and seizing funds in the name of the Reformation.

Henry divorces Catherine, who takes Mary away to raise her as a very devout Catholic. Henry has already secretly married Anne because three months after the divorce Anne gives birth—to a girl, Elizabeth.

Further arguments with Rome cause Henry to appoint himself Supreme Head of the Church of England, and Thomas More is executed for not acknowledging Henry's position.

## Yet another wife

Anne has a second child. It does not live. After only three years, Henry has tired of her and again looks for another queen. As a divorce is too complicated, Anne is charged with ridiculous offences and executed, leaving Henry free to marry Jane Seymour.

Interestingly, despite the fact that Henry is persecuting both Protestants and Catholics, Henry is still regarded by the people as a strong King and he is generally popular.

To Henry's relief, Jane soon gives birth to a boy, Edward, then sadly dies ten days later.

## Henry gets worse

Cromwell is losing favour with Henry, and to try and improve his standing, he suggests a political marriage to the German Anne of Cleves. Henry sees an attractive portrait and agrees to marry Anne, but when she arrives, Henry is so disappointed that the marriage is annulled. Anne is pensioned off and happily lives in England for the rest of her life. Cromwell is executed.

Henry is getting very odd and unpleasant when he marries wife number five, the seventeen year old Catherine Howard. Sadly, Henry finds he is not Catherine's first boyfriend and to public disgust he has her quickly executed.

Henry is old, bald, diseased and finally married to Catherine Parr, who has already been widowed twice. In 1547 he dies, passing the throne on to his son, Edward VI.

## ACKNOWLEDGEMENTS

I'd like to express my thanks to both the original production companies for their assistance in finalising this script, and especially to my wife Bridget who supports me in everything.

Kjartan Poskitt

# ACT I

*... in which we hear about the new King*

*A solemn procession moves to the stage. This includes Henry, the News-*
*reader, a Reporter, Peg, Maud, Joan, the Tutor, the Sports Reporter, and*
*other members of the crowd*

*A bell slowly chimes*

*During the following song, Henry the Eighth is crowned*

**Song 1: The Coronation Song**

**All** (*singing*) At the altar candles burn
Prayers are whispered in concern
Slowly tolls the lonely bell
As we bid our King farewell
Like the tide departs the shore
Ever to return once more
Though a sorry day
Life has passed away
and the King has gone
As his spirit flies
out to paradise
here the crown moves on...

God rest the old King and God bless the new
Angels protect him in all he may do
Hear us, oh Father, and help him, we pray
As he leads us all, as he feeds us all
Ev'ry part of the day.

God rest the old King and God bless the new
Angels protect him in all he may do

Guide him to victory and help him stay true
Hear the belfry ring and the choir sing
Alleluia to you
Amen.

*Everybody starts leaving*

*The News-reader is at her desk*

*A Reporter holds back Peg, Maud and Joan for an interview*

**News-reader**  Good evening, this is Tudor News reporting on April the twenty-first, fifteen o nine AD, and today's main story is that England has a new King! Henry the Eighth has automatically taken the Crown as the only surviving son of his late father Henry the Seventh. As the royal procession moves away from Westminster Abbey, we can go over live to find out what the public know of their new King.

**Reporter**  (*to the three ladies*) Ladies, if I can trouble you, what are your first impressions of the new King Henry?

**Peg**  He seems all right. He's like his grandad Edward the Fourth.

**Maud**  Well, that's better than being like his uncle Edward the Fifth!

*The ladies laugh morbidly*

**Reporter**  Why?

**Maud**  Edward the Fifth got murdered when he was twelve.

**Peg**  Him and his little brother, suffocated to death.

**Maud**  And you call yourself a news reporter!

*Joan always talks rather spookily*

**Joan**  In years to come, they'll be known as the princes in the tower.

**Peg**  Oh, dear, she's looking into the future again.

**Reporter**  Can she do that?

**Peg**  She never stops. It gets on your nerves.

**Reporter**  So, you're saying that Henry the Eighth's uncle was one of the princes in the tower?

**Peg**  Catch on quick, don't you?

**Maud**  Poor little Edward. It must be awful to be King when you're twelve.

**Peg** Especially if straight away somebody goes and murders you.

**Maud** He never had any fun, did he? He didn't get to have a war with France, or chop anybody's heads off, or anything.

**Reporter** So do you think this new King will have some fun?

**Peg** Not half!

**Maud** He's a bit of a laugh, is Henry.

**Reporter** It seems that he's going to be popular, then.

**Joan** Underneath his pleasing exterior lurks a diabolically self-centred fiend.

**Peg** She's doing it again!

**Reporter** So there you have it, nice guy or diabolical fiend, time alone will tell.

*With the News-reader are the Tutor and the Sports Reporter*

**News-reader** With us now is the King's private tutor. What can you tell us about him?

**Tutor** Extraordinary. He came top in French, top in Latin, top in Spanish, top in music, top in art, top in poetry, and top with distinction in scripture.

**News-reader** How many people were in the class?

**Tutor** Only one. I was his private tutor.

**News-reader** So coming top doesn't count for much, then.

**Tutor** Don't you believe it. He's quite brilliant.

**News-reader** Right, well, we take a break now from Henry, as we go to our sports desk.

**Sports Reporter** Indeed, some results just come in... The All England Tennis championship has just been won by Henry the Eighth. The Open Hunt challenge trophy has also been won by Henry the Eighth, and a late result: we've just heard that the national jousting shield has been won by—Henry the Eighth.

**News-reader** Thank you, but now we go live to Westminster to hear Henry make his first public appearance as King.

SCENE 2

*... in which the King meets his subjects*

*A big fanfare is sounded*

*Henry, Wolsey, the Scholar, Empson and Dudley, the Peasant, two heavies, some girls, and the rest of the crowd enter*

**Page 1**  Silence for the King!
**Page 2**  Silence for the King!
**Page 3**  Silence for the King!
**Henry**  Ladies and gentlemen...
**Page 4**  Silence for the King!
**Henry**  When you're ready! Thank you. Now then, you know me. For eighteen years I've been your good old Prince Henry, or Hal to my mates! Top sportsman, musician *extraordinaire*; I go to mass five times a day, and I'm fluent in several languages including, dare I say— French!

*Everybody spits on the floor*

Let's face it, when I was prince we did have a bit of fun. The trouble is, now I'm a King I'm afraid a bit of fun is now out of the question.

*The crowd sigh*

Instead we are going to have a *lot* of fun!

*The crowd cheer*

Take my father, Henry the Seventh, God rest his soul——

**Crowd**  Amen.
**Henry**  As I was saying, my father was a bit on the boring side. Apart from counting money, the only fun he had was burning Lollards.
**Peasant**  Anybody who doesn't stick to the Catholic faith wants burning.

*The crowd agree*

**Henry**  Absolutely, but that's small stuff. For instance, have we had a decent war recently?
**Crowd**  *No!*
**Henry**  Dead right, yet just across that channel, you all know what's there.
**Crowd**  *France!*

*Everybody spits*

**Henry** What were you brave English hearts doing when you should have been attacking the French? Eh?

*Murmurs from the crowd*

That's right! Paying taxes. Lots of taxes. Give them the figures.

*The Scholar steps forward*

**Scholar** Royal income for the year fourteen eighty-six: fifty-two thousand pounds.

**Henry** That was twenty-three years ago: fifty-two thousand. Now then, what was it last year?

**Scholar** One hundred and forty-eight thousand pounds.

*Gasps from the crowd*

**Henry** Your taxes have tripled in twenty years! And I say that's wrong!

*Demented cheering*

So let's find out who are the leeches responsible, shall we?

*The crowd separate, leaving two of the nobility—Empson and Dudley— alone in the middle. Everybody points and jeers at them*

Aha! Well, if it isn't the Royal tax collectors, Empson and Dudley.

**Empson** We were proud to work for your father, sire.

**Dudley** And hope to be of service to you, my lord.

**Henry** Thank you, but no. I already have an employee.

*The Executioner comes on. His Warders follow merrily, wheeling a little truck with a nasty axe and a block on it*

*The Executioner passes Empson a card*

**Executioner** Ed the Head at your service. Executions and disembowelings to go. Guaranteed money back if you're not completely dead.

**Henry**  So what do we think of our two tax collectors?

|                                          | **Song 2: The Body Rock** |
|------------------------------------------|----------------------------|

**Crowd** (*chanting*)    Guilty guilty

**Empson**
**Dudley** } (*together*)    It's not fair
                            Guilty of what?

**Crowd**                    We don't care!

**Empson**
**Dudley** } (*together*)    We were only trying to follow our orders

**Crowd**                    Tough luck! Here come the warders and…

> Your body's gonna rock
> your head is gonna roll,
> Tomorrow six o'clock,
> You're gonna take a little stroll
> Put your shoulders on the block,
> start praying for your soul,
> 'Cos your body's gonna to rock
> your head is gonna roll,
> And you can't do a thing because
> that's the wish of the King.
> Oh yeah!

**Empson**
**Dudley** } (*together*)    Don't blame us for doing what we were told
                            Collecting your money, your silver and gold

**Crowd**                    You tax collectors you're all the same
                            You take everything except the blame

> Your body's gonna rock
> your head is gonna roll,
> Tomorrow six o'clock,
> You're gonna take a little stroll
> Put your shoulders on the block,
> start praying for your soul,
> 'Cos your body's gonna to rock
> your head is gonna roll,
> And you can't do a thing because

that's the wish of the *King*...
Oh, yeah!

*The Warders usher Empson and Dudley off. The Executioner follows*

**Peasant** (*shouting*) What about the money?
**Henry** Eh? What money?
**Peasant** The taxes we've been paying, are you going to give it back?
**Henry** No! We're going to need it when we attack France.

*Everybody spits*

Believe me, every single person here will be proud to be an English man.
**Heckler** (*shouting*) I'm a woman!
**Henry** You can be proud to be an English woman, then.
**Heckler** No, I can't. I'm Welsh.
**Peasant** Same thing.
**Heckler** Oh no, it isn't!
**Crowd** Oh yes, it is!
**Heckler** Come here, I'll smack the lot of you!
**Henry** Please! We'll sort Wales out later. The point is, any money spent on smashing the French is money well spent, right?

*The crowd cheer*

So that's what we'll do, then. Go on, spread the word.

*The crowd go off*

*The Peasant lingers. Wolsey sidles up to Henry*

**Peasant** Just as long as you don't spend our taxes on yourself.
**Wolsey** Allow me, sire.

*He goes and puts a friendly arm around the Peasant*

My dear peasant, maybe you'd like my assistants to explain to you the intricacies of government finance.

*Two heavies casually usher the Peasant off*

*There is a scream off stage*

**Henry** (*to Wolsey; aside*) You're a pretty smart operator.
**Wolsey** One does what one can, your grace.
**Henry** Who are you?
**Wolsey** I was a chaplain at your coronation, sire. My name is Thomas Wolsey.
**Henry** Thomas Wolsey, eh? I tell you what, I'll call you Tom. How about that?
**Wolsey** I should be delighted, your grace.
**Henry** Right, then, Tom. Anyway, I better get to church, I've only been three times today so far.
**Wolsey** But surely you have other matters to attend to?
**Henry** Too right! After church I've got the tennis court booked, then I'm composing some organ music, then I'm off hunting.
**Wolsey** But, sire, a King has obligations to his subjects!

*Some girls pass by. Henry has his eye on them*

**Girls** Coo-ee!
**Henry** Absolutely, Tom. Hallo, subjects! (*He is about to sneak off with the girls*)
**Wolsey** Sire, I beg you, there is a kingdom to run.
**Henry** If you're so keen, you do it. So, girls, who's coming to the bathroom? I'll show you my model navy.

*Henry and the girls exit*

**News-reader** And so Thomas Wolsey has now taken over a large section of the King's duties, but we have news of one duty that even Mr Wolsey cannot perform. First, though, we have an old report made in the year fifteen o one. Prince Henry, as he was then, is nearly eleven years old.


SCENE 3

*… in which Henry finds he has to marry his brother's widow*

*A group of children, led by Henry as a ten year old boy, dash on stage, finishing a race*

**Boy Henry** Hah! I win again.

**Kid** I hate playing with you. Why do you always have to win?

**Boy Henry** Because I'm a prince! Royal blood's the secret. I'm brilliant at everything. Who's for another game?

*A Nanny runs on*

**Nanny** Sire!

**Boy Henry** Oh, Nanny, what is it? Can't you see I'm busy beating everybody at everything?

**Nanny** Sire, I have news.

**Boy Henry** Out with it, then.

**Nanny** Well, sire, do you want the sad news or the glad news?

**Boy Henry** Who wants sad news? What's the glad news?

**Nanny** You have just been betrothed to be married to Catherine of Aragon.

**Boy Henry** Catherine who?

**Nanny** Of Aragon.

**Boy Henry** But my brother Arthur's married to her!

**Nanny** That's the sad news. He's just died of consumption in Wales.

**Boy Henry** But he was only fifteen!

**Nanny** That's Wales for you.

**Boy Henry** Have I got to marry her right now? I'm only ten.

**Nanny** No, but you'll have to marry her eventually. You see, when she married Arthur, her family paid your father a lot of money, and he doesn't want to pay it back.

**Boy Henry** OK, OK. I'll marry her sometime. Just as long as she isn't French!

*Everybody spits on the ground and goes off*

**News-reader** And so the question now is: will Henry try to conveniently forget about his engagement?

*A gang of court girls enter, followed by the jester Will Sommers who accosts them*

**Will** Greetings, my pretty maids! And tell me, which pair of lips would have a spare kiss for me?

**Girl 1** Oh, no! It's Will.

**Girl 2** There's no pair of lips here for you.

**Will** It does not need to be a matching pair. Your top lip and your bottom
lip will do.

**Girl 2** Oh, get lost!

**Will** Get lost? Is that any way to talk to the court jester? By my troth, I am
the wittiest fellow in Christendom.

**Girl 1** Witty? You?

**Will** Honk, bladder and cuckoo!

**Girl 3** You're about as witty as a wart.

**Will** Aha, yet in so saying, is not a wart a veritable source of wit?

**Girl 2** Oh, no, you've started him off.

**Will** Tell me, did you ever hear a wart speak?

**Girl 2** Of course not.

**Will** And so you never heard a wart utter a single dull word?

**Girl 1** Oh, dear.

**Will** In faith, then, if a wart never utters a dull word, and I am like a wart,
then I must be a merry fellow indeed!

*The girls stare at him blankly*

**Girl 2** Why?

**Will** For you see, like the wart, I never utter a dull word! Now, for my wit
I demand a kiss.

**Girl 1** There's an old cart-horse outside.

**Girl 2** Yes, why don't you kiss that?

**Girl 3** Make sure you get the right end.

**Will** Hah! You all think you save your kisses for King Henry! Well, save
them indeed, for as old maids you shall live to regret their accumulation!

**Girl 1** What is he on about?

**Will** Our lord approaches. Silence, and you shall learn.

*The girls all bow flirtingly*

*Henry marches on, talking to Wolsey*

*As he talks, Henry sits down and the girls immediately start pandering
to him*

**Henry** Catherine *who*?

**Wolsey** Catherine of Aragon, your grace. You have been betrothed to her these seven years.

**Henry** Oh, you mean Spanish Catherine.

**Wolsey** Indeed, a delightful woman, she'll make you a fine Queen.

**Will** Sire, if she can make you a fine Queen, do you think she could make one for me while she's at it?

*Henry laughs. Indeed Henry is the only person in the world who finds Will funny. The girls suddenly join in laughing with Henry. As soon as he stops, they stop*

**Wolsey** Terribly witty, I'm sure, sire, but you must realise the throne needs an heir.

*Will plucks a hair from his head*

**Will** If the throne needs an 'air it can have one of mine!

*Henry laughs again. The girls have to laugh too. Wolsey smiles thinly*

**Henry** Ladies, are we not fortunate to have such a funny fellow as Will amongst us?

**Girls** Oh yes, sire!

**Wolsey** Sire, though my ribs ache from mirth, the country needs to know who is to be its next King.

**Henry** What do you mean the *next* King? I've only been here seven weeks. That's charming, that is. Thanks a bunch.

**Wolsey** Sire, the security of the Crown would be assured if you had legitimate male offspring.

**Will** Never mind about male offspring... I'm a male on a spring! Boing boing boing... (*He jumps around*)

*The girls automatically laugh, but Henry is too deep in thought*

**Wolsey** Ahem!

*The girls suddenly stop laughing. Meanwhile, Henry has figured it out*

**Henry** In other words, if Catherine's the Queen and we have a son, then everybody'll be happy, right?

**Wolsey** Your grace has cracked it.
**Henry** Oh, go on, then. She's not a bad sort. Sorry, girls, I've got to go
and marry Catherine of Aragon.

*Girls all moan a bit*

Hey! I'll be back. In the meantime Will will keep you happy.
**Will** Will will, my lord! Will will!

*Henry and Wolsey exit*

*Will turns to the girls*

Will will, will Will!
**Girls** *Shut up!*

*Will exits*


**Song 3: I Wanna Be Queen!**

**Girl 1**      When I was only small I didn't know at all
What I wanted to be
Days that I would wish of being a fish
or just a bumble bee

*Other girls mutter that she must be a bit soft in the head*

But now that I am older my plans are rather bolder
And so I did decide that
The ultimate thing is for the King
to choose me as his bride...

*Other girls agree and join in*

**Girls**      I wanna be Queen
Yes I do yes I do I do
You know what I mean
Guess you do I guess you do
I'm terribly keen

It's so true it's so true it's true
I wanna be Queen
    Yes I do yes I do
I don't need expensive presents from a far off shore
just a crown will do with a palace or two
I won't ask for more
I wanna be seen yes I do yes I do I do
being the Queen you know it's true...
        I'd keep myself tidy from my head to my toes
        I'd shave my legs and powder my nose
You know what I mean
I'm terribly keen
I wanna be Queen!

I wanna be Queen
    Yes I do yes I do I do
You know what I mean
        Guess you do I guess you do
I'm terribly keen
        It's so true it's so true it's true
I wanna be Queen
    Yes I do yes I do
When I sunbathe in the garden on a summer's day
I always wish someone'd take my picture
Half a mile away
I wanna be seen
        Yes I do yes I do I do
being the Queen you know it's true...
        I'd be regal majestic and great
        I'd only execute the people I hate
You know what I mean
I'm terribly keen
I wanna be Queen—wah wah wah wah
You know what I mean
I'm terribly keen
I wanna be Queen!

*The girls depart sulking*

SCENE 4

*... in which Henry gets an invitation*

*Henry is posing for a portrait, which is being painted by Holbein*

**News-reader** Tudor News now reports from the year fifteen twelve AD. King Henry has been on the throne for three years, and as I speak, he is about to receive some encouraging news from his wife.

**Henry** Make sure you've got my legs in, they're gorgeous, my legs. Look!

**Holbein** Be still, be still, be still!

**Henry** I want to check, let me see.

**Holbein** Not till I finish. Be still.

**Henry** Charming! I bring you all the way from Switzerland, and you won't show me what you're up to.

*Catherine of Aragon (who is Spanish, remember?) comes in*

**Catherine A** 'Enry! It is there are you. Hola!

**Henry** Hallo, Catherine.

**Holbein** Still, I say!

**Henry** This chap Holbein won't let me see his picture of me.

**Catherine A** It I can see. Oh, he got your left ear right.

**Henry** He's got my left ear right? So where's my right ear, then?

**Catherine A** Your right ear—it right 'ere!

**Henry** Hah! You jest! I love a good jest, me.

**Holbein** You moved!

**Catherine A** 'Enry, papa have something for me to asking you.

**Henry** Your father? Old Spanish Ferdinand of Aragon? What does he want?

**Catherine A** He want to attack the south of France.

**Henry** Who doesn't?

*Both spit*

**Catherine A** He ask, you can send an army to join with him and biff up the Frenchmans, if you like.

**Henry** Good old Ferdinand. Biff up the Frenchmans? Of course I like! Come on, let's go and tell the lads, they will be pleased.

**Holbein** Be still!

*But Henry dashes off, followed by Catherine*

(*He mutters*) Just for that I'm going to make you look *fat*.

*He exits*

*During the News-reader's speech, some bored Soldiers enter and stand to one side of the stage*

**News-reader** Tudor News can now report that the English army are assembled down on the Spanish-French border, and we have our war correspondent Lady Adie on the spot.

*Lady Adie approaches one soldier*

**Lady Adie** Hi! I'm reporting for Tudor news.
**Soldier 1** Aren't you Lady Adie?
**Lady Adie** Yes, but you can call me Kate. So where's the fighting? I love a bit of blood and guts.
**Soldier 2** Huh! We haven't had the orders yet.
**Lady Adie** But you've been here for months.
**Soldier 1** Tell us about it! We're still waiting for Ferdinand to give us the go-ahead.
**Lady Adie** So why doesn't he?
**Soldier 1** He's letting his Spanish boys have all the fun.
**Soldier 2** Yeah, they're having a right old ding-dong while we're just stuck here in the rain.
**Soldier 3** Brothers, I move that we should organise a mutiny.
**Lady Adie** A mutiny?
**Soldier 1** Good idea. It's chucking down with rain.
**Lady Adie** That's no reason to mutiny!
**Soldier 2** A lot of us have dysentery.

*He rushes off urgently*

**Lady Adie** That's no reason to mutiny!
**Soldier 3** We've run out of beer.

**All**  *What?*
**Lady Adie**  That's official, then. It's *mutiny!*

*All disperse*

*During the News-reader's speech, Henry and a sculptor, Pietro Torrigiano, enter*

**News-reader**  Thank you, and we go straight back to the palace to see the reaction to this news.

*Henry is slowly and patiently explaining some drawings to Pietro*

**Henry**  This is a drawing of my father Henry, see? And this is one of my mother, Elizabeth.
**Pietro**  Que?
**Henry**  I want you to use these drawings... Yes...? To design one of your nice memorial tombs—or gravestones if you like... To go in the Henry the Seventh chapel in Westminster Abbey.
**Pietro**  Que?

*Catherine A arrives in a temper*

**Catherine A**  'Enry!
**Henry**  Oh, not now, Catherine.
**Catherine A**  *'Enry! Pedazo de animal!* Now you do listen to *me!*
**Henry**  Yes, dear.
**Catherine A**  Que te as creido que eres? Papa complain your army they have mutinied!
**Henry**  Serves him right. They've been sitting in a muddy field for months; he won't give them the signal to join in.
**Catherine A**  Stupido! 'E was just going to! 'E turn round to say "OK, Englishmans, go biff Frenchmans"—but no, they all gone off, for to find a pub, for to drink beer.
**Henry**  Really?
**Catherine A**  Papa say next time he biff Frenchmans, you not invited.
**Henry**  Oh, come off it——
**Catherine A**  Papa esta cabriado! Is how you say, gone flippin' mental.
**Henry**  Oh... OK! Tell old Ferdinand that he can cut the throats of any English soldiers caught deserting.

**Catherine A**  Oh, bueno! Is nice! Mucho gracias, my dear darling dumpling bum!

*Catherine showers a very embarrassed Henry with kisses and then exits*

*Henry turns to Pietro*

**Henry**  Foreigners! Don't they just get on your nerves?
**Pietro**  Que?
**News-reader**  We now bring you a report from the following year, fifteen thirteen AD. Once again, France is under attack from Henry in the north and Ferdinand in the south.

*A messenger runs on with a piece of paper and hands it over—or an arrow with a message plunges into the desk!*

Correction, we've just heard that Ferdinand has pulled out, but the English are still on the attack and are being led into battle by King Henry himself. That's quite extraordinary! We can now go straight back to our war correspondent in northern France...

*Lady Adie enters*

**Lady Adie**  I wouldn't bother, there's still no blood or anything. Here we are all ready for a decent fight and the French have disappeared.

*A lot of very boisterous Soldiers come on jeering*

**Soldier 1**  Come back and fight!
**Soldier 2**  Cowards!
**Soldier 3**  Run home to mummy!
**Lady Adie**  Aha, here comes the King. Maybe we'll find out what happened.

*Everybody goes quiet*

**Henry**  Gentlemen! Please, may I just say, I think the French all deserve gold medals.
**Soldier 2**  Medals? They all ran away!
**Henry**  I know, and anybody who can run that fast deserves a medal.

**Soldier 3** We hardly even saw them.

**Henry** Indeed, all we saw of them was their spurs. As a consequence I shall call this battle "The Battle of the Spurs"!

*Huge laugh*

(*Modestly*) It wasn't that funny.

*The laughter suddenly stops*

No, seriously, chaps...

*He unfolds a note to read, as music starts for:*

### Song 4: The Battle Of The Spurs

The French all say they're sorry but they've something else to do
They've gone off to the doctors and joined a massive queue
Some complain of cold feet, others feel so weak
but most of all their backs all seem to have a yellow streak!

**Soldiers** We came to fight the mother of a battle...
we came to give the French a bit of stick,
but once they heard the English sabres rattle
most of them were violently sick.
We came to lay the countryside to ruin
But off they ran and left us all with nothing doing
They always were pathetic, but now they're worse
Since the Battle of the Spurs!

*Music continues*

**Henry** You know what, chaps? Being King can be a long, tough, dirty job, but it's days like this and guys like you that make it all worthwhile, and I mean that.

*Big cheer*

**Soldiers**     We're going to send a message and we're going to make
                 it clear
                 France has really had it 'cos we're English and we're
                 here!
                 No one's going to stop us, the French are in the bag
                 We're going down to Paris now to fly the Royal flag...

                 We came to fight the mother of a battle
                 We came to beat the French up fair and square
                 But off they ran like herds of frightened cattle
                 They wish they'd stayed at home to wash their hair

                 The King of France can hardly hide his blushes
                 Half his men are throwing up behind the bushes
                 They always were pathetic, but now they're worse
                 Since the Battle of the Spurs!

*All march off*


SCENE 5

*... in which Wolsey gets promoted*

*Wolsey is sitting, doing some bookwork. In attendance are two of his big
thugs*

**News-reader** Next, we catch up with the situation three weeks later at the
palace. Wolsey has been in charge.

*Will waltzes in, trying to be funny*

**Will** Ah, Wolsey! What a sad fellow are you.
**Wolsey** Silence or die.
**Will** Such authority, and yet I am about to see you bow before a hen that
will never lay an egg!

*Wolsey lethargically clicks his fingers and a thug moves over to beat up Will*

(*Hurriedly*) Hen-ry!

*Wolsey and the thugs are suddenly alert*

**Wolsey**  The King?

*Henry enters*

*Wolsey hurriedly rises to his feet*

**Henry**  Ah, Tom, I see Will is keeping you amused. Just as well, because you've missed all the fun.
**Wolsey**  Really, your grace?
**Henry**  You bet. We've just sent the French packing.
**Wolsey**  Oh, splendid, sire. All we had here was an invasion from Scotland.
**Henry**  Invasion from Scotland? Come off it! King James the Fourth married my sister Margaret. He's not the invading type.
**Wolsey**  He isn't now. He's dead.
**Henry**  Dead? James? How come?
**Wolsey**  I told you. He invaded and Lord Surrey stopped him at the border. They had a simply ghastly battle at Flodden field, and James was slain. It was all terribly messy.
**Henry**  Well! Nice one, Tommy! I tell you what, how do you fancy being my chief minister?
**Wolsey**  Oh, top hole!
**Henry**  You can be Lord Chancellor too, if you like.
**Wolsey**  Lord Chancellor? I say!
**Henry**  In fact, why not have the full set? You're a churchy type, how does Archbishop of York sound?
**Wolsey**  York?
**Will**  You know, nice place up North, quite near Bridlington, if you fancy a day at the seaside.
**Wolsey**  Oh. It's just that I'd always rather fancied Canterbury.
**Henry**  Don't be greedy. Besides, old Archbishop Warham's still there, he crowned me and he did my wedding to Catherine, you know. York's nice, you can have York.
**Wolsey**  You're more than kind, your grace.
**Henry**  There's just one thing. You keep calling me your grace.
**Wolsey**  Your grace?
**Henry**  There was a chap in France called "Maximilian the Holy Roman Emperor". It's got a certain swing to it, don't you think?

**Wolsey** You wish to be called that?

**Henry** No! Just something better than "your grace". Even little bishops get called that. I'm a King.

**Wolsey** How about—your highness?

**Henry** Your highness? What do you think, Will?

**Will** Your highness? It suits you, sire, because you are amongst the tallest in the land, and in being tall, so you are indeed high!

*Henry laughs uproariously at this doubtful attempt at Shakespearean humour*

**Henry** Ha! What a funny fellow you are. You must stay and amuse Tom while I go and amuse my dear Catherine.

*Henry exits*

*Wolsey eyes Will coldly, but Will does not care*

**Will**                    There is an Archbishop of York,
                        Who grunts when he's trying to talk,
                        with a small curly tail,
                        he stinks without fail,
                        no wonder, he's made out of pork!

*Will skips around stupidly and accidentally bumps into the thugs*

*Suddenly he stops laughing as they drag him off for some implied unpleasantness*

**Wolsey** Only a fool makes enemies when he should be making friends.

*He exits*

SCENE 6

*… in which Henry starts a family*

*Catherine of Aragon is lying down, with the women around her. Joan has a strangely shaped bone which she dangles from a thread over Catherine's stomach*

**News-reader** But now we move on two years to November fifteen fifteen, and we go straight to the Queen's bedchamber.

**Catherine A** Tell again! You are right, yes?

**Peg** Go on, Joan, try again.

**Maud** She's never wrong, you know.

**Joan** The Queen will give birth on the eighteenth of February.

**Maud** If that's what she says, then it must be right.

**Peg** It gets on your nerves.

**Maud** Hush! Here comes the King.

*Joan quickly pockets her bone and they all stand back guiltily*

*Henry enters*

**Henry** My dear Catherine, you look faint.

**Catherine A** Is not faint! Oh, no, is not faint 'Enry the papa.

**Henry** Papa? Me?

**Catherine A** I have a pregnant.

**Henry** Pregnant? Poor Catherine, not again! How many times has this been?

**Catherine A** 'Enry, this time is different. This child will live.

**Henry** How do you know? What witchcraft has been practised here?

**Catherine A** 'Enry! Women do know these things. This child will live!

**Henry** We must think of a name. Henry! There's a good name.

**Catherine A** No. Little Henry has been.

**Henry** But that was five years ago, and he only lived ten days...

**Catherine A** Only? *Only?* Ten days was a lifetime for my son Henry. I not have another Henry.

**Henry** I'm sorry, Catherine.

**Peg** How about James?

**Henry** A bit Scottish.

**Maud** George?

**Henry** A bit German.

**Peg** Francis?

**Henry** Sounds a bit like France!

*Everybody spits*

**Maud** Dwight P Shultzman!

**Henry** Sounds a bit American.

**Maud** American?

**Henry** You know, that new place Columbus discovered somewhere near Ireland. Catherine, I know! We could name him after his brother.

**Catherine A** Que?

**Henry** Call him Henry Junior!

**Joan** The child will be called Mary.

**Henry** Mary? But that's a funny name for a boy...

*Black-out or similar abrupt ending*

*The Latin Correspondent enters during the Black-out*

*The Lights come up again*

**News-reader** But indeed on February the eighteenth the following year, Catherine did give birth to Princess Mary. Meanwhile, Thomas Wolsey is getting very powerful. The Pope has made him a cardinal, and now, in fifteen eighteen, the Pope has given him the powers of "Legate a latare". Our Latin correspondent will now explain.

**Latin Correspondent** Wolsey could tell the Archbishop of Canterbury what to do.

**News-reader** Was that it?

**Latin Correspondent** Pretty well.

**News-reader** So there you have it. Moving on to fifteen twenty, we find Cardinal Wolsey is ridiculously powerful, but at the same time incredibly stylish.

*Wolsey approaches Henry, who is looking at some plans*

**Wolsey** You wish to see me, my lord?

**Henry** Yes, Tom, I do. Where's the money I wanted for my new Royal Navy?

**Wolsey** Sorry, my lord, I've been a bit busy fixing this peace treaty in France...

**Henry** *France? (He spits)*

**Wolsey** Relax! Believe me, you'll love it!

*A Master of Ceremonies, waiters, maids, and other party people come on*

### Song 5: Wonderful Waste Of Time

**Master**      Cardinal Wolsey cordially requests you join him down in
          France
with a glittering gang of guests giving peace a chance
Everyone is going to see the English in their prime
hosting what is going to be
Wolsey's wonderful waste of time

**All**      Though it's true for a minute or two,
we must discuss defences
it's just a trick so we can stick
the whole thing on expenses

Down at the Field of the Cloth of Gold
all the heads of state
will dance away as stars unfold
and eat from silver plate
As elegant ladies by the score
admire the view sublime
we'll drink champagne galore
At Wolsey's wonderful waste of time

You'll see royalty let down their hair
so rave on everyone you've got to be there

Down at the Field of the Cloth of Gold
we're going to turn them green
when we show them how to hold
the smartest party seen

As music plays the night away
and midnight starts to chime
The world will not forget the day
of Wolsey's wonderful waste of time.

You'll see royalty let down their hair
so rave on everyone you've got to be there.

As music plays the night away
and midnight starts to chime

The world will not forget the day
of Wolsey's wonderful
wonderful wonderful waste of time...!

*Everybody exits*

**News-reader** Henry was also impressing people. Even the Pope was pleased with him.

*The Pope strolls on and calls up his assistant Cardinal Guiseppe*

**Pope** Hey, Guiseppe!

*Guiseppe enters*

**Guiseppe** You wanna me?
**Pope** Gimme the truth. This Henry of England, he a good guy, no?
**Guiseppe** He not bad.
**Pope** I see he wrote a book about what a slimeball Martin Luther is.
**Guiseppe** I not read it.
**Pope** You wanna read it. Is good! And tell me, does he still burn Lollards?
**Guiseppe** Of course he burn Lollards! He only human.
**Pope** I gotta name for him, then. Tell Henry I call him "Fidei Defensor". Is a good name, eh?
**Guiseppe** Is a—very good! OK, I tell him.

*They stroll off amicably*

**News-reader** For a translation of "Fidei Defensor", we once again turn to our Latin correspondent.
**Latin Correspondent** "Defender of the Faith".
**News-reader** That's the Pope's new title for the King, is it?
**Latin Correspondent** Yup.
**News-reader** You don't say much, do you?
**Latin Correspondent** No.

*During the News-reader's speech, Will and a Doctor enter*

**News-reader** Well, anyway, that was five years ago and now we are approaching Queen Catherine's fortieth birthday. Henry's hopes of her having a son are fading.

*The Doctor is putting some rather unnerving tools back into his bag. They include a huge bloody saw, a drill, etc. Will approaches him*

**Will** Why, it is the ugly doctor! Thou must indeed be a rich man.
**Doctor** Why, Fool?
**Will** Fie, the sight of thy face maketh everyone sick, therefore thou hast the more to cure!
**Doctor** Well, if you're sick, take one of these.

*Will takes something from a jar and pops it in his mouth*

**Will** Forsooth what kind of pill is this?
**Doctor** That was no pill, that was a leech.

*Henry enters*

**Henry** Good doctor, you have examined the Queen. What news?
**Doctor** I am sorry, sire, but Queen Catherine will never bear you another child! I have tried—(*he pauses a second as he wields a horrible saw/drill/pincers-looking device and packs it*) everything!

*He shuts his bag and exits*

**Henry** But what am I going to do? There has to be a son to carry on the line.


SCENE 7

*… in which Henry's eye starts to wander*

**News-reader** Despite his eighteen happy years of marriage to Catherine, Henry's desperation caused him to take notice of a new arrival at court.

*Henry, Anne Boleyn, and all the Courtiers come on*

*The song features Anne Boleyn playing a mean lute*

**Song 6: Six Finger Annie**

**Courtiers**     Get the word, in the street
The palace is a-poppin' to a brand new beat
There's a girl both sweet and smart
About to take this place apart

The court is thumping
the crowd are jumping
when she gives her lute that rock and roll
She hits those stringers
with extra fingers
and plays so tight you just might lose control

She can shimmy like her sister Maggie
She can boogie all night long
She can sing out the blues all raggy
She can really kick the gong
        She's fun she's fair she's fine of figure
        And her left hand is just a little bit bigger
Six finger Annie can really rock a lute along

She's got—ooo-wah—personality
she's got—ooo-wah—sensuality
with her speciality abnormality
of her extra digitality
*What* you *what* you *what?*

They call her sin'ster
across Westminster
with that bad time boogie that she brought
She gave them hassle
Down Windsor castle
and caught the guard off guard at Hampton Court.

She can shimmy like her sister Maggie
She can boogie all night long
She can sing out the blues all raggy
She can really kick the gong
        She's fun she's fair she's fine of figure

> And her left hand is just a little bit bigger
> Six finger Annie can really rock a lute along
>
> She's got—ooo-wah—personality
> she's got—ooo-wah—sensuality
> With her speciality abnormality
> of her extra digitality
> *What* you *what* you *what*
> Let's hear what she's got!

*There follows a wicked lute instrumental*

> She can shimmy like her sister Maggie
> She can boogie all night long
> She can sing out the blues all raggy
> She can really kick the gong
> > She's fun she's fair she's fine of figure
> > And her left hand is just a little bit bigger
> Six finger Annie can really rock a lute along

*Everybody exits, leaving Henry alone*

**Henry** (*to the audience*) That woman will become my Queen even if I have to move heaven and earth to do it!

*During the News-reader's speech, Wolsey and a Scholar with a Bible enter and join Henry*

**News-reader** Henry had suddenly become very determined, as Thomas Wolsey was to find out.

**Wolsey** Sire! You cannot marry Anne Boleyn, you are married to Catherine.

**Henry** But Catherine cannot have a son! Is that my fault? Now be a good lad and pop off to the Pope and arrange me a divorce.

**Wolsey** But the Pope might not play along!

**Henry** Of course he will. I'm his Defender of the Faith. If I'm defending his faith, he owes me one. Besides, he allowed my sister Margaret a divorce from her second husband.

**Wolsey** Sire, the Pope will need an absolute corker of a reason.

**Henry** Give him the absolute corker.

**Scholar** Leviticus Twenty—Twenty-one.

**Wolsey** Leviticus? But that's in the Bible!

**Henry** You bet it's in the Bible. Listen——

**Scholar** Picture the scene: God was having a chat with Moses——

**Wolsey** I am aware of Leviticus.

**Henry** Tell him what God said.

**Scholar** "And if a man shall take his brother's wife it is an unclean thing——"

**Henry** Catherine was my brother Arthur's wife, remember?

**Scholar** He goes on to say: "and they shall be childless."

**Henry** There you are. The reason I never had a son was that we were never legally married.

**Wolsey** But sire, you have a daughter, Mary!

**Henry** Tom! I don't want conversation about this, just *fix it*!

<br>

SCENE 8

*... in which we meet Princess Mary*

*Catherine, Mary and some other women are sitting doing some needle-work*

**News-reader** We now take a break to catch up with Catherine and her teenage daughter. Henry has sent them away hoping that they will be forgotten, but instead they have found a great deal of public sympathy.

**Mary** (*throwing her sewing away; suddenly*) Oh, Mother, what are we going to do?

**Catherine A** Shhh, Mary!

**Mary** Shhh? How can I? Father is saying he never married you, which makes me illegitimate.

**All** Shhh!

**Mary** He is! Just because he wants to get his hands on that eleven fingered strumpet, Anne Boleyn.

**All** Shhh!

**Catherine A** Please, Mary, we must be hush!

**Mary** Why?

**Catherine A** Because we are women and the men are in charge. It is how it has always been.

**Mary**  Well, I think it's time a woman took over.

*A small cheer from the assembly*

### Song 7: Do Your Worst

**Mary** ⎫ (*together*)  Day and night you see us sitting
**Cath** ⎭                  working at our needles and our knitting
                             waiting for our lives to slowly waste away
                             Henry should be getting nervous
                             wond'ring how he could deserve us
**Mary**                     'cos I'm going to see that he pays one day.

**All**                      Mary Mary see they don't forget
                             The way you've been mistreated
                             the reason you're upset
                             Mary your blood is blue
                             Mary your crown is due
                             Mary go and do your worst.

**Mary**                     I'm going to show the house of Tudor
                             a woman can be rougher, can be ruder
                             I will not be locked away to disappear.

**All**                      No more sex discrimination
                             Time that a woman ran the nation
                             The meanest thing they've seen since Boadicea is
                                 here.

                             Mary, Mary, see they don't forget
                             the way you've been mistreated
                             the reason you're upset
                             Mary your blood is blue
                             Mary your crown is due
                             Mary go and do your worst.

                                 By the light of flaming martyrs
                                 she'll sign her royal charters
                                 undoing everything her father's done.

And as heretics are burning
the world will all be learning
a daughter is as strong as any son.

No more commiserating,
soon we'll be celebrating
the day when Mary Tudor comes to take the crown
Men that under-rate us
with secondary status
will get a shock when Mary knocks them down
down down.

Mary, Mary, see they don't forget
the way you've been mistreated
the reason you're upset
Mary your blood is blue
Mary your crown is due
Mary go and do your worst.

That's why on the throne
Mary you will be known as
Bloody Mary the first.

*Henry comes in with warders*

**Henry** What is going on here?
**Mary** You have no right to treat us like this. I am a princess and one day
  I shall be the Queen.
**Henry** You are not a princess, you're just trouble.
**Mary** I am, and my mother is the Queen.
**Henry** What have you been telling her?
**Catherine A** I tell nothing!
**Henry** Take her away. Stick her in a convent or something. From now on
  she never sees her mother again.

*The warders grab Mary, who screams*

**Mary** You'll be sorry!
**Henry** Say goodbye to your mother.

**Mary** You can't do this! You can't!
**Henry** *Shut up!*

*The warders drag Mary off, but not without getting severely bitten, kicked and scratched in the process. Catherine wails and rants*

**Henry** (*shouting*) Oh, don't you start! How come you people can't be quiet and sensitive like me?

*Henry exits*

*Catherine is lead away sobbing*

SCENE 9

*... in which Wolsey lets Henry down*

**News-reader** Meanwhile, in the Vatican, Pope Clement the Seventh has had a message from Thomas Wolsey.

*The Pope strolls on with Guiseppe, who has presented the Pope with a form to sign*

**Pope** So! Henry wants a divorce, eh?
**Guiseppe** It not really divorce; Henry just want you to agree he no really marry Catherine in the first place. He want you to sign here.
**Pope** Is he still a good guy, this Henry?
**Guiseppe** He still burns Lollards.
**Pope** Is good. OK, where do I sign?

*Charles the Fifth storms in*

**Guiseppe** Blimey! It Charles the Fifth of Spain, your holiness.
**Charles** Que passa aqui? What all this I hear about Henry divorce my aunty Catherine?
**Pope** She's your aunt?
**Charles** Is my aunt and is the Queen of England and is going to stay that way.

**Pope** Hey! Cool it, Charles, Henry not a bad guy, he make sure Catherine will be OK.

**Charles** *Con mucho cuidado!* You forgetting I do run Italy as well as the Spain right now! I can make the Vatican is bad, bad place to live.

**Pope** Oh yeah, yeah, yeah.

**Charles** Before you say "yeah, yeah, yeah", don't forget that I got a new system starting up, it called the Spanish Inquisition.

*Guiseppe lets out an involuntary shriek. The Pope sheepishly tears up the form*

**Pope** (*muttering nervously*) Hey, what are friends for, eh?

*They exit*

**News-reader** We now have a reaction from the palace.

*Henry storms on, followed by an apologetic Wolsey*

**Henry** How can Charles stop me divorcing a woman to whom I've never been married?

**Wolsey** I'm afraid the Pope does what Charles tells him, sire.

**Henry** So why doesn't the Pope do what you say? You've got the biggest mouth in Europe.

**Wolsey** Really, sire, I have tried——

**Henry** Tried? Rubbish! All you ever do is go round building things. You build universities, you build palaces, you even built Ipswich! What did you want to go and build Ipswich for?

**Wolsey** Sire, let me go back to York, and I'll give your position some serious thought.

**Henry** Oh, really? If that's the best you can do, maybe I should give *your* position some serious thought.

*Wolsey exits*

Honestly, what happened to the old Tom I used to know? Where will I find another like him?

*Cranmer, More and Cromwell suddenly appear*

**Cromwell** Coo-ee!
**Henry** Who are you?

**Song 8: The Three Toms**

**Courtiers**    This is Tom, this is Tom
This is Thomas too
Have no fears for the next few years
they'll run the place for you
They got brains they got muscle
they got reputation
They're just the thing to help a King to
organise his nation.

First up prepare to meet a really clever guy
Thomas Cranmer fixes things like you eat apple pie
There's no problem on this earth that he can't understand
Have no cares the state affairs are solid in his hand.

This is Tom, this is Tom
this is Thomas too
Have no fears for the next few years
they'll run the place for you.

Next up is Mr Nice known as Thomas More
any time of day or night you're welcome at his door
He's the one to stick around when others run away
and if you all go out to lunch he'll be the one to pay.

This is Tom, this is Tom
This is Thomas too
Have no fears for the next few years
they'll run the place for you.

Last up, Thomas Cromwell likes to get respect
anyone who messes him is seriously wrecked
He don't take no nonsense, *no!*
He's bad, he's mad, he's mean
Trouble just evaporates once this man has been
because

This is Tom, this is Tom
this is Thomas too
Have no fears for the next few years
they'll run the place for you.

This is Tom, this is Tom
this is Thomas too
Don't be so grand hold out your hand
and say *how do you do*!

*Everyone exits*

*An instrumental version of* The Body Rock *(available on the backing tape) starts up. After a few seconds the music is faded to a lower level to allow the News-reader to announce:*

**News-reader** And so with the arrival of the Three Toms, we conclude Part One! Meanwhile, you'll be wondering, what will happen to Thomas Wolsey? Will Henry really marry Anne Boleyn? If so, what will happen to Catherine? What will happen to her daughter Mary? Will there ever be a prince and what can the Pope do about it? Part Two contains all the answers as well as multiple wives, burnings, beheadings and the complete Reformation of the church as we know it. Join us in fifteen minutes after the break!

*The music is faded back up to play out the end of Act I*

# ACT II

## Scene 1

*... in which Henry's new advisers take over*

*The beat starts for Song 9*

**News-reader** Welcome back. It's now the year fifteen thirty and you join us just in time to see a rather unwelcome group of visitors call on Cardinal Wolsey in York.

*The Executioner and a gang of warders drag Wolsey on*

**Song 9: The Body Rock**

**Executioner**    Wolsey, Wolsey, what ya going to do?
                    The King has sent me to come and get you.
**Wolsey**         You daren't touch me, you haven't got the power!
**Warders**       Don't you believe it, you're going to the tower and—

*As they sing, they load him on to the Executioner's truck and wheel him round*

**All**              Your body's gonna rock
                    your head is gonna roll,
                    Tomorrow six o'clock,
                    You're gonna take a little stroll
                    Put your shoulders on the block,
                    start praying for your soul,
                    Your body's gonna rock and
                    your head is gonna roll,
                    And you can't do a thing because
                    that's the wish of the King.

**Wolsey**         *Stop,* you fools, you don't understand!
                    I'm Lord Chancellor of this land.

**Warders**        Wolsey, Wolsey, we told you before
                   Henry gave your job away to Thomas More.

                   Your body's gonna rock
                   your head is gonna roll,
                   Tomorrow six o'clock,
                   You're gonna take a little stroll
                   Put your shoulders on the block,
                   start praying for your soul,
                   Your body's gonna rock and
                   your head is gonna roll,
                   And you can't do a thing because
                   that's the wish of the King.

**Executioner**    Hold it everybody! He doesn't look well.
**Warders**        He always looked horrible, how can you tell?
**Executioner**    Look!

*The song abruptly stops*

He's dead!
**Warder 1** Where are we?
**Warder 2** We've only got to Leicester.
**Warder 1** Poor bloke, missing his own execution.
**Executioner** Yeah, he'd have been right cut up about it if he was alive.
**Warder 1** He'd have been well gutted.
**Warder 2** He'd have been mortified.

*And with these choice observations they haul Wolsey off*

*During the News-reader's speech, the Reporter, More, Cromwell,
Henry, and the Warders enter. Henry carries an axe*

*They assume their positions: More and Cromwell sitting unhappily, each
restrained by a Warder, holding his shoulders. Henry is pacing about
flexing the axe, like a schoolmaster flexing a cane*

**News-reader** We now take you to fifteen thirty-two, and the tension is
mounting. Henry has been waiting five years to marry Anne Boleyn and

to make things worse, Anne is not as amenable as all the King's other girlfriends! Indeed, Anne is bravely withholding her favours until she is married. We now hear from our reporter on location in the court.

**Reporter** You don't! I'm not going in there. He's gone mad, he's like a different man.

**News-reader** Oh.

**Henry** I'm asking for the last time, and if I don't get answer, then your neck's next. *Cromwell!*

**Cromwell** Me, sire?

**Henry** You, tell me how I can force the Pope to agree to a divorce.

**Cromwell** Well, obviously you deserve a divorce, sire, seeing as how you're such a brilliant and popular King and all that...

**Henry** Undo his collar.

*The Warder bares Cromwell's neck*

**Cromwell** Sire!

*More laughs gloatingly*

**Henry** Shut up, More. What have you got to offer?

**More** Er...

**Henry** Undo his too.

*Cranmer comes in and puts down a suitcase*

**Cranmer** Sorry I'm late, sire.

**Henry** Where have you been, Cranmer?

**Cranmer** I've just spent five years in Europe, sire.

**Henry** Well, Mr Thomas Five-Years-in-Europe Cranmer, you now have five seconds to tell me how I can get a divorce.

**Cranmer** Ignore the Pope, just do it.

*Henry laughs a little. He then laughs a lot. In relief everybody joins in*

**Cromwell** Good one, sire. Like it, like it.

*Henry suddenly stops laughing and explodes*

**Henry** *Is that it?* After *five years* all you can say is "Ignore the Pope"?

**Cranmer** Yes, sire.

**Henry**  Before we throw some daylight on your adam's apple, let me explain why you are an imbecile. If I ignore the Pope, nobody will recognise my second marriage and consequently Anne's sons will never be Kings.

**Cranmer**  You're wrong, sire.

**Henry**  Did you say I'm *wrong*?

**Cromwell**  He did, sire, I heard him.

**More**  (*to Cromwell*) Belt up, before we all cop it!

**Cranmer**  Sire, I've visited most of the top brains in Europe and they can't stand the way the Pope's letting Charles of Spain boss him around.

**Henry**  Go on...

**Cranmer**  Here's the good bit! They agree that you were never married to Catherine in the first place.

**Henry**  Really?

**Cranmer**  They're on your side, so as I say, ignore the Pope.

**Henry**  I like it!

*Will dashes on, clutching something behind his back*

**Will**  Sire, I bring sad news and glad news.

**Henry**  What's the sad news?

*Will produces the Archbishop's hat from behind his back*

**Will**  Your dear friend Archbishop Wareham has just died.

**Henry**  Oh. Poor old Wareham, he was a dear friend.

**Cromwell**  Oh, yeah, shame, he was a great bloke. You're right there, sire.

**More**  (*aside*) I think I'm going to be sick.

**Will**  But, sire, the glad news is that—Archbishop Wareham has just died!

**All**  Eh?

**Henry**  Brilliant!

**Cromwell**  Yeah, brilliant! I never liked him.

**Henry**  Didn't you?

**Cromwell**  No—yeah? No, I mean, well, I didn't like him—but in a likeable sort of way...

**Henry**  In the corner, Cromwell. Now!

*Cromwell goes to stand in the corner. Henry then turns back to Cranmer*

You see, Tom, sad though it is to lose old Wareham, that does mean

there is a convenient vacancy. How would you like to be the Archbishop
of Canterbury?
**Cranmer** Nice!

*Henry passes Cranmer the Archbishop's hat*

**Henry** Right, Archbishop Tom, your first job is to get me divorced.
**Cranmer** No problem.

*More whimpers slightly*

**Henry** What is it, More?
**More** If you get divorced, the Pope won't like it, sire.
**Henry** More, have you been listening? We're ignoring the Pope. We're
England! We're not going to be dictated to by some foreigner.
**More** He's not some foreigner, he's the Pope. We're all good Catholics,
remember?
**Henry** I know, I'm a brilliant Catholic, but the Pope doesn't count
anymore, not according to some of the biggest brains in Europe.
**More** In that case, sire, I resign.

*More stomps out*

**All** (*childishly*) Woooo! Temper, temper!
**Henry** That's enough, settle down.
**Cromwell** Aren't you going to chop his head off, sire?
**Henry** No, Cromwell, I am not.
**Cromwell** Why not?
**Henry** Because at least he's honest, Cromwell. Now then, I'm going to
need another chancellor.
**Cromwell** Oh, please, sire, me, sire!
**Henry** Are you a good Catholic?
**Cromwell** The best.
**Henry** But exactly what are your feelings regarding the Pope?
**Cromwell** (*carefully*) He needs help. He just hasn't got the feel for this
country. In fact, I feel that our branch of the Catholic church could best
be served by an independent Head of the Church of England.
**Henry** But who could do that? I've run out of people called Tom.
**Cranmer** Anne Boleyn's father's called Tom. Sir Thomas Boleyn.

**Henry** It'd look like a bit of a fix.

**Cromwell** Sire! There's only one man for this job. You do it, you'd be brilliant!

**Cranmer** (*aside to Cromwell*) You *are* a creep!

*Cromwell smiles smugly at Cranmer*

**Henry** But what happens if all the bishops and people don't agree?

**Cromwell** I'll have a word with them, sire, it'll be my pleasure.

*Everybody comes on to be addressed by Cromwell*

### Song 10: Rise Up

I'm gonna tell a sad story,
About the country we love
We're in the hand of an alien land
and we say enough is enough.

**Cromwell**
**Cranmer** } (*together*) Too long we've been wasting
In the shadow of Rome
Now's the hour take the power
and bring it back on home.

**All**   *Rise up*, you're gonna hear the
*Cry's up*, we're gonna light the
*Skies up*, so dry your
*Eyes up*
Reformation's what you need.

We always did what they told us
since the Bible began
Now we've seen what fools we've been
Tell the Vatican.

We're gonna
*Rise up*, you're gonna hear the
*Cry's up*, we're gonna light the
*Skies up*, so dry your
*Eyes up*

Reformation's what you need.

*The music speeds up and people start getting frenzied*

> We're gonna give the church a crashing
> *Rise! Rise!*
> We're gonna start the statue smashing
> *Rise! Rise!*
> We're going to burn
> All they made us learn
> Rise up Rise up
> Rise up Rise up
> Rise Rise Rise Rise Rise...

*The music reverts to a more respectable pace*

> We don't need us a leader
> we got a man on the throne
> So let the Pope sit prettily down in Italy
> We got a pope of our own.
>
> *Rise up,* you're gonna hear the
> *Cry's up,* we're gonna light the
> *Skies up,* so dry your
> *Eyes up*
> Reformation's what you need!

**Henry** So now, does anybody object if I allow myself a divorce?
**All** No, sire.
**Henry** Thank God for that!
**Cranmer** I'll be able to marry you to Anne Boleyn now.
**Henry** Er, yes, to be honest, we already secretly got married in January.
**Cranmer** Why?
**Henry** Because we had to! Now, come on, we've got to move fast.
**News-reader** And so, on May the twenty-third, fifteen thirty-three, Henry was finally divorced from Catherine. A week later, on June the first, Anne was crowned Queen to mixed approval.

SCENE 2

*... in which Henry finds that marrying Anne brings its problems*

*A crowd, including Maud, Joan, and Peg, is watching the wedding procession*

**Crowd** Long live the Queen! Long live the Queen!

**Maud** I don't think it's right, you know.

**Peg** I know, poor old Queen Catherine. I feel really sorry for her and Mary.

**Maud** They say they've both turned very religious.

**Peg** Can you blame them?

*Cromwell approaches*

**Cromwell** You're not cheering much.

**Maud** Long live the Queen.

**Peg** Happy now?

**Maud** I tell you what. Queen Anne looked a bit fat in that dress.

**Cromwell** Watch it! That's my mate's new wife you're talking about. Anyone who upsets Henry, upsets me.

**Maud**
**Peg** } (*together*) Oo-er, get you!

**Joan** The Queen is not fat.

**Cromwell** See? You want to listen to your friend here.

**Joan** The Queen is expecting a child.

**Peg** No! Are you sure?

**Maud** Don't say that Henry's been putting his cakes in before he bought the oven.

**Cromwell** That remark is treasonous!

**Joan** The Queen will give birth in three months' time.

**Peg** She's always right, you know.

**Maud** Three months, eh? That's a bit quick. So how do *you* explain that?

**Cromwell** Er... If the King wants to produce a baby in three months, he can! He is, after all, the King.

*Cromwell stomps off haughtily*

**Maud**
**Peg** } (*together*) What a creep!
**Joan**

*They exit sniggering*

**News-reader**  We now take you to the palace about three months later, on
September the seventh...

*There is a scream of panic and some courtiers and attendants run across
from Henry who comes on with the Midwife. He is withholding his
temper*

**Henry**  What do you mean, "it's a girl"? Have you looked?
**Midwife**  Yes, sire.
**Henry**  Have you looked very carefully?
**Midwife**  Yes, sire.
**Henry**  Nothing's fallen off?
**Midwife**  Sire?

**Song 11: Blue**

**Henry**                 There's a little blue cot in the nursery
                          with a little blue blanket or two,
                          And of course a little wooden horse
                          also painted blue.
                          There's a blue pair of curtains at the window
                          and a blue rug on the floor
                          and if you care to look
                          there's a little blue hook
                          to hang things on the door

*The Courtiers arrive to sing the backing*

| | |
|---|---|
| **Courtiers** | Bal-loo-oo |
| **Henry** | it's a pretty colour |
| **Courtiers** | bal-loo-oo |
| **Henry** | I don't want any other |
| **Courtiers** | bal-loo-oo |
| **Henry** | the only one that will do |
| **Courtiers** | bal-loo-oo |
| **Henry** | I like it glossy or matt |
| **Courtiers** | bal-loo-oo |
| **Henry** | I would even paint the cat |
| **Courtiers** | bal-Ioo-oo |
| **Henry** | pander my compulsion |

slap on the emulsion
save me from convulsion
any other colour gonna
fill me with revulsion.

**Courtiers**  There's a little blue table in the nursery
with a little blue table cloth too
Standing there is a little high chair
of a similar hue
There's a little blue plate and a little blue cup
and even a little blue spoon
**Henry**  and if I had my way, at the end of the day
**Courtiers**  there'd be a blue moon.

Bal-loo-oo
**Henry**  it's a pretty colour
**Courtiers**  bal-loo-oo
**Henry**  I don't want any other
**Courtiers**  bal-loo-oo
**Henry**  the only one that will do
**Courtiers**  bal-loo-oo
**Henry**  I like it glossy or matt
**Courtiers**  bal-loo-oo
**Henry**  I would even paint the cat
**Courtiers**  bal-loo-oo
**Henry**  pander my compulsion
slap on the emulsion
save me from convulsion
**Courtiers**  any other colour gonna
fill him with revulsion.

There's a little blue cupboard in the nursery
with a little blue laundry bag too
There's a whole lot more in every drawer
painted bal-loo...

**Henry**  Yes, blue is my favourite colour
and that's why I think
I'm going to faint now I'm having to paint
everything pink.
**All**  Ah-bal-oo!

**Midwife** I'm glad you've taken it so well.

**Henry** *Aaarghh! (He throws a fit)*

*Everybody skedaddles, leaving Henry with Cranmer*

**News-reader** Disappointment indeed, but after this unwelcome news, Henry has to receive an equally unwelcome visitor.

*Guiseppe comes in grinning*

**Guiseppe** King Henry, hi! I gotta the message for you from the Pope. By the way, I sorry to hear about the little girl.

**Henry** What about her?

**Guiseppe** You know! In Italy we got a word for kid whose parents, they not married.

**Henry** Anne and I are married.

**Guiseppe** Oh, no. The Pope he say you still married to Catherine.

**Cranmer** No, he isn't. I gave him a divorce.

**Guiseppe** Ah! You the Archbishop, eh? Boy, have I gotta news for you! You don't count no more.

**Cranmer** I don't count?

**Guiseppe** No. The Pope excommunicated you. *(To the audience)* Boy, some days I love this job!

**Henry** He can't excommunicate my Archbishop!

**Guiseppe** And—the Pope says he gonna excommunicate you too.

**Henry** *Me?*

**Guiseppe** That was the message.

**Henry** Was it? Was it really? Well, he can't excommunicate me. Do you know why?

**Guiseppe** Do I look like I care?

**Henry** I'm changing my title. I'm now *Supreme Head of the Church of England!* Got that?

**Guiseppe** The Pope, he ain't gonna like that.

**Henry** So? Over here I *am* the Pope. If Clement wants to excommunicate me, then I'll excommunicate him first.

**Guiseppe** OK. Bye-bye, little King. And good luck. You gonna need it.

**Henry** You'll need it!

*Some tough types enter and close in around Guiseppe*

*He is not at all bothered*

**Guiseppe**  Hey! Watch it, I got connections in the Spanish Inquisition.

*He is hurriedly released and he casually walks off*

**Henry**  Supreme Head of the Church of England! Good title, eh? Let's make it official. Let's call it the Act of Supremacy, that should make it clear enough.

**Cranmer**  Some of the monks and monasteries won't be too pleased, Your Highness.

**Henry**  So? (*He shouts off*) Tom!

*Cromwell comes on*

Tom, tell Tom about your plan. (*To Cranmer*) Listen to Tom, Tom.

**Cromwell**  Well, Tom, I'm shutting down abbeys, churches, monasteries, you name it.

**Henry**  And...

**Cromwell**  Selling them off, smashing them up, basically privatising them and pocketing the profits.

**Henry**  Ahem... Not pocketing! We're re-investing in a stable monarchy, all together now...

**All**  For the good of the country.

**Henry**  Everybody in the land has to realise that I am now in sole charge.

**Cromwell**  Everybody apart from Sir Thomas More, of course.

**Henry**  Oh, yes? What about Tom, Tom?

**Cromwell**  It's just, well, he still says that the Pope's in charge of the church.

**Henry**  Oh, no, there's always one, isn't there?

**Cromwell**  Of course, a trip to the Tower might change his mind.

**Cranmer**  The Tower? But Sir Thomas is one of your best friends!

**Cromwell**  That's why we're helping him be a loyal subject, isn't that right, Your Highness?

**Henry**  You're right, Tom. It'll be for his own good.

**Cromwell**  You're too kind, Your Highness.

*Cromwell exits smugly*

*Henry is absorbed in thought*

*Will enters*

**Henry**  Highness? You know what, Tom, I'm getting bored of being my highness. I need a better name.
**Cranmer**  Really, Your Highness?
**Henry**  *Tom!* Are you deaf? I said I was *bored* of highness!
**Cranmer**  Your worship?
**Henry**  Hmmm, better, but not quite me.
**Cranmer**  Magnificence?
**Henry**  Getting warmer...
**Cranmer**  Your majesty?
**Henry**  Sounds good... Ah, Will, what do you think?
**Will**  But, sire, it is the name of a common woman.
**Henry**  Who?
**Will**  The good wife Esty. By her first name she is known as Madge.
**Henry**  Madge Esty? There can't be two of us! Have her burnt.
**Will**  Sire! It was a jest.
**Henry**  Would you make a jest out of the name of the King?
**Will**  Well, there is a jest in the name, your ma-jest-y. Ha ha... Ha?
**Henry**  You've stopped making me laugh, Will.

*All but Henry scuttle away*

**News-reader**  This is an urgent announcement. The public are warned that the King is becoming increasingly unpredictable. Whether you are noble or peasant, you are advised to take the utmost care when dealing with His Highness——

*Henry draws an axe on the News-reader, who hurriedly corrects herself*

I mean His Majesty!
**Henry**  (*to the audience; ranting*) It's pathetic, isn't it? Peasants can have sons, serfs can have sons, dogs, mice and fish can have sons, but not me.
**News-reader**  Sadly, Henry will never know how great a queen his daughter will become.

*Joan, the news team and anybody else available come on to sing*

### Song 12: Big Bessie
**All** (*singing*)    Big Bessie Big Bessie
                       Big Bessie Big Bessie...

Big Bessie you better believe
is better than a baby boy
when Bessie is queen it's gonna have been
the best time we could ever enjoy.

Big Bessie you better believe
will be the backbone of the land
when she's a little bit older she's gonna be the holder of
Europe in the palm of her hand.

> But Bessie beware your daddy don't care for you
> a boo hoo hoo
> He's gonna make your mother
> try to have another
> 'cos only a brother will do.

Big Bessie you better believe
will be the best thing in her day
You're gonna hear the cheers for forty-five years
Big Bessie rules OK.

Big Bessie you better believe
will be brilliant by and by
Big Bessie oughta be the little daughter
who's the apple in her daddy's eye.

Big Bessie you better believe
won't be beaten by the bully Boys
and she'll even get harder when the Spanish
    Armada
finds that Bessie makes the biggest noise.

> But Bessie beware your daddy don't care for you
> a boo hoo hoo
> He's gonna make your mother
> try to have another
> 'cos only a brother will do.

Big Bessie you better believe
will be the best thing in her day

You're gonna hear the cheers for forty-five years
Big Bessie rules OK.

*They all exit*

*The Lights dim to represent a dank prison cell*

*More enters, to position himself in a corner, shivering and in chains*

*The Executioner ushers Cromwell on stage*

**Executioner** Sir Thomas is this way, sir. Mind the rats.

*Cromwell swaggers towards More, then holds his nose to indicate a bad smell*

**Cromwell** Ah, Tommy More! How's life in the tower?
**More** Absolutely fine.
**Cromwell** Really? We freeze you, we starve you, we took away your books, we took away your family——
**More** But still you can't take away my faith! You don't like that, do you? I still believe in the Holy Church of Rome, and there's nothing you can do about it.
**Cromwell** Oh, I don't know. It's very hard to believe in anything when— (*he produces a death warrant*) you haven't got a head.
**Executioner** Gadzooks! He signed it, then?
**Cromwell** Yes, Tom, the King has finally signed your death warrant.
**Executioner** But I thought you and Henry were friends?
**More** His majesty does me a favour. To live in the same world as Mr Cromwell has never been a privilege.

*The Executioner sniggers rudely at Cromwell, then turns back to More*

**Executioner** We're going to miss you round here, Sir Thomas. I'll get my best axe polished up for you.
**Cromwell** And what difference does that make?
**Executioner** I wouldn't like Sir Thomas to catch any germs off it while he's being executed.

*The Executioner turns to More and tries to be pleasant*

Well, sir... See you in the morning.

*The Executioner starts to leave with Cromwell, who mockingly starts to sing*

**Cromwell** (*singing*) Your body's gonna rock
                            your head is going to roll...

*Just as Cromwell goes off we see the Executioner deftly trip him up or give him a little push*

*There is a scream and a crash off stage*

**Executioner** Do watch out for the stairs, sir.

*The Executioner and More exit*

*During the News-reader's speech, Henry enters and is pacing up and down*

**News-reader** We now move into fifteen thirty-six with news that the queen is expecting another child. Everybody from barons to beggars is hoping and praying the child will be a boy.

*Will is roughly pushed on to the stage. He is very, very nervous*

*Cromwell and Cranmer are lurking nearby*

**Henry** You have news?

*Will tries to be jolly*

**Will** Indeed, sire. I have sad news but also glad news.
**Henry** Sad news?
**Will** The child did not live.

*Henry stares at him dumbstruck*

But, but the glad news... It was a boy! Ha ha ha ha?

*Will suddenly panics completely and runs out of the theatre never to be seen again*

**Henry** Cromwell, Cranmer, here!

*Cromwell and Cranmer come on from where they have been lurking*

What am I to do?

**Cranmer** The Queen is yet young. She can try again.

**Henry** She's tried for three years. Useless! I have to have a son.

**Cromwell** Of course you do, sire.

**Henry** Which is why it's time for me to take a different wife.

**Cranmer** Another one?

**Cromwell** Have you got some lucky girl in mind, then?

**Henry** Of course. *Next!*

*Jane Seymour comes on*

(*He mutters*) Thomas Cromwell, Thomas Cranmer, meet Jane Seymour.

**Cranmer** Charmed...

**Cromwell** Delighted...

**Henry** Shut up, you two. Jane, do you think you could bear me a son?

**Jane** I don't know, my lord.

**Henry** Go on, I'll make you Queen first.

**Jane** Thank you, my lord.

**Henry** Fine. Tom, give me a divorce and I'll marry Jane here.

**Cranmer** But sire, I need a reason!

**Henry** *What?*

**Cranmer** Just the merest little hint of a reason, for appearances sake. Last time we had Leviticus on our side.

**Henry** But Anne has to go! Of course it's not for me, you understand, it's...

**All** For the good of the country.

**Cromwell** Does it have to be divorce?

**Henry** How do you mean?

**Cromwell** Suppose she was found guilty of incest and adultery, you could have her executed.

**Henry** Incest and adultery? But Anne doesn't go round committing incest and adultery.

**Cromwell** She doesn't have to. We can still make a court find her guilty of it. After all, who's everybody's favourite King round here?

**Henry** You dare to suggest that we execute my wife? An innocent woman?

*Cromwell is nervous. However, Henry chuckles horribly*

I like it! All I need to do to get a new Queen is chop the head off the old one. What do you think, Jane?

*Jane is rather worried*

Cheer up! Give me a son and you won't have a thing to worry about.

*Cranmer leads away the uncertain Jane*

**Cranmer** It's all go, isn't it?

*They exit*

*We see a courtroom of people arrive, headed by two ushers*

### Song 13: The Body Rock

**Ushers** (*chanting*) Silence silence
                silence silence
                Silence silence, the court will rise,
                here comes the Judge to lead the assize.

**Jury**          We've heard all about your dirty misdemeanours,
                Stand by, Anne! You're going to the cleaners and your...

**Judge**        *Silence!* Silence, stop the uproar
                this is supposed to be a court of law
                Now Anne, your case is despicably severe
                Is there anything you think we really ought to hear?

**Anne Boleyn** I have listened to your charges
                I know they're all a lie
                It's just for the King's convenience
                that I should have to die
                First you swore upon the Bible,

these crimes were true of me
so now all of you must realise,
you're damned eternally...

*Jurors look uncomfortable*

**Judge**          Members of the Jury you must take a care
                   that the trial is just and the punishment fair
                   But most of all I hope you all know
                   The King won't be happy if you let her go!

**Jury**           Have no worries, we won't fail,
                   English Justice will prevail.

**Judge**          So give me the verdict,
                   what do you say?

**Juror 1**        Guilty
**Juror 2**        Guilty
**Juror 3**        Guilty
**Juror 4**        Guilty
**Juror 5**        Guilty
**Juror 6**        Guilty
**Jury** (*all together*)    Take her away...

*The Executioner comes on merrily*

**All**            Because your body' s gonna rock
                   your head is gonna roll,
                   Tomorrow six o'clock,
                   you're gonna take a little stroll
                   Put your shoulders on the block,
                   start praying for your soul,
                   Your body's gonna rock
                   your head is gonna roll,
                   And you can't do a thing because
                   that's the wish of the King...
                   Oh, yeah!

*All exit*

*Joan rushes on, disturbed*

**News-reader**  We now have a paranormal update from the Court Clairvoyant.

**Joan**             The body of the Queen still walks,
                       seeking for her head,
                       And round the tower it still will walk
                       when all we here are dead.

**News-reader**  Indeed, despite losing her head, Anne Boleyn is destined
to be active for hundreds of years, and who can blame her? Within
twenty-four hours of her execution, Archbishop Cranmer was heard to
say...

**Cranmer**  Henry of England and Jane Seymour, I now pronounce you
man and wife. You may kiss the bride... Oh! Could someone pick His
Majesty's clothes up?

SCENE 3

*... in which Jane pays dearly for Henry's good news*

**News-reader**  And from that scene of gaiety we move on to October.

*A mass of Courtiers creep on softly and start singing*

Song 14: It's A Boy

**All**             Whisper if you dare,
                      the nation is at prayer,
                      with just one thing upon its mind
                      the palace shut today
                      and the crowd was kept away
                      as the doctor and the midwife,
                      with the queen have been confined...

*The Doctor and the Midwife come on*

**Doctor**  ⎫
**Midwife**  ⎬  (*together*) It's a boy—
**All**                                             it's a boy!
                      At last the King is father of a boy...

Shout for joy, shout for joy
It's a boy it's a boy it's a boy...

Sound the bell, sound the bell
There's a waiting nation we must tell
All is well, all is well
Sound the bell sound the bell sound the bell...

Lord, be ready to guide him
Lord, be there to provide him
for the crown to come.

Sing a song, sing a song
to the Prince for whom we've waited for so long
Sing it strong sing it strong
Sing a song sing a song sing a song.

Lord, ever be next him
Lord, ever protect him
for the crown to come.

It's a Boy, it's a Boy
At last the King is father of a boy...
Shout for joy, shout for joy
It's a boy, it's a boy it's a boy...

*Everybody marches off singing*

*The music continues but fades as we realise that Jane has been left on stage. She is lying motionless. The Doctor and Midwife are at her side*

**Midwife**      My lady? Lady Jane?

*The Doctor quietly draws a sheet over Jane's head*

*End of music*

**News-reader**  Tragically Jane died twelve days after giving birth to
Henry's son. Details of Edward now from our Court Clairvoyant.

**Joan**         The son that Jane has died to give,
is very weak but he shall live,

to take the throne at ten years old,
then six years later die of cold.

SCENE 4

*... in which Cromwell finds himself in trouble*

**News-reader** Thank you, and now back to Henry. Aside from married
life, he has been spending more and more time building up the Royal
Navy, and consequently he has left Thomas Cromwell rather to his own
devices.

*The Reporter catches Thomas Cromwell*

**Reporter** Hallo, Mr Cromwell. Tudor News here, can I ask you how the
Reformation is going?
**Cromwell** Not too bad. Churches have been smashed up, piles of money
collected, we're well ahead with the suppression of the Catholics...
Basically it looks good.
**Reporter** Do you realise that Henry thinks you're taking it too far?
**Cromwell** Wimp.
**Reporter** But people are starting to blame Henry for what you are doing.
**Cromwell** Well, deary me! Poor old Henry.
**Reporter** But surely he might execute you?

*Henry creeps up behind Cromwell*

**Cromwell** Henry? Execute me? He wouldn't dare.
**Henry** Oh, wouldn't I?
**Cromwell** Sire! What an unexpected pleasure! And you're looking so
well, how do you do it? Oh, by the way, I've got to tell you, that song
of yours, *Greensleeves*, I can't stop singing it. Great tune, good beat...
Funny, I was just saying to Tom Cranmer, we're lucky to have such a
brilliant King...
**Henry** *Shut up!*
**Cromwell** Shut up, sire? Me, sire? What a good idea, sire.
**Henry** I leave you in charge of a little thing like the Reformation and you
go completely mad, and now you think I daren't execute you. Ed!

*The Executioner comes on with his Warders*

*The Executioner makes preparations for executing Cromwell. This includes measuring his neck, setting out the block, and doing a few practise swings of the axe*

**Cromwell** But, sire, I've been doing lots of other things! I've even got you another wife lined up; you like having wives, remember?
**Henry** Idiot, who needs a wife? I have my son.
**Cromwell** Sire, this one's different. She's German, and if you marry her, the Germans will join you to fight the Pope and everybody.

*The Executioner is just about to raise his axe. Henry pauses him*

**Henry** A German? What's she like?
**Cromwell** Would I let you down, sire? This way everybody!

*A whole load of jolly Germans conveniently arrive to slap their thighs, clap their hands and sing*

**Song 15: Wunderbar Anne**

**Germans**          We sing a song about Anne of Cleves
Wunderbar wunderbar Anne!
the finest girl to ever breathe
Wunderbar wunderbar Anne!
          No-one holds a candle to this lady of the Rhine
          next to her the sun can hardly shine
Truly then you must believe
you're such a lucky man
if you marry Anne of Cleves
Wunderbar wunderbar Anne!

**Henry**            What does she look like?

**Germans**          When she is walking across the land
Wunderbar wunderbar Anne!
Children all run up to hold her hand
Wunderbar wunderbar Anne!
          Her laughter is so lovely it can light up any room
          she can bring a garden into bloom—bloom
          bloom

Truly then you must believe
you're such a lucky man
if you marry Anne of Cleves
Wunderbar wunderbar Anne!

**Henry**          That's fine, but I still don't know what she looks like!

**Germans**     Always kind and tries to please
Wunderbar wunderbar Anne!
Ever so clean and she never has fleas
Wunderbar wunderbar Anne!
    The only time she makes us sad is when she has
    to go
    Mein Gott, how our tears all flow—flow—flow
Truly then you must believe
you're such a lucky man
if you marry Anne of Cleves
Wunderbar wunderbar Anne!

**Henry** Lovely, fine, super, smashing, ten for personality, *but* what does she look like?
**Cromwell** Look at this, sire.

*Cromwell passes a small portrait to Henry*

**Henry** Cor!

*During the News-reader's speech, a huge crowd, including the Judge, gathers around Henry to wait expectantly*

**News-reader** And so in fifteen thirty-nine Henry went to meet Anne at Rochester.
**Henry** Which one is she?

*Some German courtiers turn up ushering Anne of Cleves, who has a bag over her head*

Oh-oh! I've got a bad feeling about this.
**German** May I present the German, Anne of Cleves.

*Henry approaches her cautiously. Anne has her back to the audience.*
*Henry raises the bag. He gulps awkwardly*

**Anne of Cleves**  Hallo.
**Henry**  Oh, no!

*Henry lowers the bag on Anne's head again*

**Cromwell**  No? But officially, you've already married her.
**Henry**  You're joking! *Next!*
**Cromwell**  The Germans think she's gorgeous.
**Henry**  Let the Germans have her back, then.
**Cromwell**  But, sire… If you send her back, then Germany will probably
join everybody else against you.
**Henry**  Anne, nothing personal, but you're not my type. However, I tell
you what, I'll treat you like my own sister, you can have a pension, and
live here as long as you like.
**Anne of Cleves**  Thank you. I shall live here until fifteen fifty-seven when
I shall die of old age.
**Henry**  My word, you Germans are organised.

*Anne and the followers exit, leaving Henry and Cromwell and the crowd*

**Cromwell**  Well done, sire, you handled that brilliantly, as usual.
**Henry**  You tried to set me up, didn't you?
**Cromwell**  No!
**Henry**  Admit it, it was a practical joke, wasn't it? Big laugh, dragging me
down here with your fancy pictures.
**Cromwell**  I did it for the good of the country!
**Henry**  You think playing jokes on your King is for the good of the
country?
**Cromwell**  No!

*The Judge steps from the crowd*

**Henry**  Oh, come on, I like a joke, too. Try this one…

      **Song 16: We Know You Like A Laugh, Mr Cromwell!**
**Judge**         We know you like a laugh Mr Cromwell
         So we've gone to great expense

to fix a trial that'll make you smile
as you answer in defence
**Jury**    We know you like a laugh Mr Cromwell
so you'll have a good time in court
when you hear all the various invented and hilarious
charges that we've brought——

**All**    Woah woah woah *One*
**Judge**         —you ruined most of the land
in the King's own name.
**All**    Dooby dooby dooby *Two*
**Judge**         —your Reformation's out of hand
and Henry's had the blame.
**All**    Deebee dee *Thu-ree* three a tee hee hee...
**Judge**         —and the one to seal your fate
was embarrassing
**All**    embarrassing
embarrassing the King
with a very bad blind date.

We know you like a laugh Mr Cromwell
and yet you show dismay!
Is something wrong?
Your face is so long
What have you got to say?

**Cromwell**    Sire, I've been your right-hand man
I'm your very best friend your number one fan
**Henry**    Yes, Tom, that's very true
**All**    But just for once the joke's on you
'Cos...

Your body's gonna rock,
your head is gonna roll,
Tomorrow six o'clock,
you're gonna take a little...

*Henry suddenly interrupts, the music continues quietly in the background*

**Henry** Hang on! Tom, you're not singing! Don't say you don't know the words, you of all people. Tom, sing it for me nicely. Go on, very nicely, who knows, you might put me in a good mood.

**Cromwell** Sire...!

**Henry** Get on with it, tomorrow at six o'clock, what are you going to do?

*Cromwell stumbles his way through the chorus rather feebly*

| | |
|---|---|
| **Cromwell** | Take a little stroll... |
| **Henry** | Very good. Now then, where are you going to put your shoulders? |
| **Cromwell** | Put my shoulders on the block... |
| Henry | And? |
| **Cromwell** | Start praying for my soul, |
| | because my body is going to rock |
| | and my head is going to roll, |
| | And I really can't do a thing because... Because... |
| **Henry** | Tell him everybody! |
| **All** | You can't do a thing because |
| | that's the wish of the *King...* |
| | Oh Yeah! |

**Henry** So what do we all think?

*The crowd all boo and the Executioner merrily steps forward*

Bye-bye, Tom.

*The Executioner leads Cromwell away, followed by the crowd*

(*He laughs to himself*) Now that's what I call a joke!


SCENE 5

*... in which Henry tries yet again for the perfect wife*

*Henry is sitting bored, with Cranmer beside him. One by one, the court women—Agnes, Gwyneth, Sharon, Mildred and Catherine Howard—will pass before him*

**News-reader** It seems Cromwell was right about one thing. Henry liked having a wife, and his court was always full of eligible young women...

**Henry** *Next!*

**Mildred** My name is Mildred, I'm sixteen years old and come from Lincoln. If I was Queen, I'd like to travel the world and do a lot of charity work.

**Henry** *Next!*

**Agnes** My name is Agnes, I'm eighteen years old and my hobby is weaving undergarments from peacock feathers.

**Henry** *Next!*

**Gwyneth** My name is Gwyneth, and I'm forty-eight years old——

**Henry** *Next!*

**Gwyneth** But I can tap dance!

**Henry** *Next!*

**Sharon** My name is Sharon——

**Henry** *Next!*

**Catherine H** My name is... My word, but you've got nice legs.

**Henry** What?

**Catherine H** Forgive me, my Lord, but I couldn't help but notice. And what a lovely beard, too.

**Henry** You think it suits me?

**Catherine H** It makes the King of France's beard look like a warthog's bottom, my Lord.

**Henry** Such brains! Such perception, such good taste! Where were you when I first got married?

**Catherine H** I don't know, my Lord. It was thirteen years before I was born.

*Cranmer noisily stifles a snigger. Henry gives him a murderous look, then turns sweetly back to Catherine*

**Henry** Do go on, my dear...

### Song 17: This Time It's For Real

**Catherine H**  Whenever I hear you I feel I could fly
just to be near you brings a tear to my eye
I don't have an ambitious plan
I don't see the crown I just see the man

**Henry**  Can it be true she doesn't care about wealth?
It's something quite new, I'm being loved for myself.

**Henry**
**Catherine H**  } *(together)* So at the altar we're going to kneel
This time we know it's for real!

**All**         Rise and shine and crack the wine
                Everyone it's wedding time
                and this time we know it's for real
                At last the King has passed the ring
                to the one he'll adore
                Together forever
                they'll live evermore.

                Weddings come and weddings go
                but this one's really going to show
                a love that's too strong to conceal
                            In years to come when they get old
                            and nights are long and days are cold
                            their hearts will be enshrined in gold
                as this time we know it's for real.

*Music continues*

*Cranmer is standing in front of Catherine and Henry, who are being
nauseatingly lovey-dovey*

**Cranmer**  Henry, do you take this woman——
**Henry**  To be my lawful wedded wife, blah blah blah, I do.
**Cranmer**  And do you, er—sorry, I didn't catch your name.
**Catherine H**  Catherine Howard.
**Cranmer**  Thank you, Catherine Howard, do you take this man——
**Henry**  (*very quickly*) To love, honour, cherish, obey, worship, serve,
   adore, oblige, and generally fantasise about? Yes, she does, don't you?
**Catherine H**  Er...
**Henry**  She does!
**Cranmer**  I now pronounce you——
**Henry**  *Man* and *wife*!

*The crowd cheer*

*Guests file up to pay respects*

**Guest 1**  Congratulations, my Lord.
**Henry**  Thank you.

**Guest 2** May you both be very happy.
**Henry** Thank you.
**Guest 3** Well done, my Lord, I know she'll give you a good time.
**Henry** What?
**Guest 3** I—I said, "I know she'll give you a good time"!
**Henry** How do you know?
**Guest 3** She gave me one.

*Sudden ominous change of music*

*The Executioner enters*

**Henry** Catherine...?
**Catherine H** My lord?
**Henry** Take her away.
**Executioner** She's only seventeen!

*Henry scowls horribly*

**Catherine H** Do what you have to do. I am not afraid.

*The Executioner leads Catherine away*

*The crowd hiss quietly. Henry fumes at them*

**Henry** *Silence!* How dare you all? Am I not the *King*?

*The crowd all file away silently*

*End of music*

*The Executioner comes to the front of the stage wiping his axe. A couple of warders come on with him*

**Executioner** Ladies and Gentlemen, if you don't mind, we just wanted to have a quick word about what we do. You see, this used to be such a great job, didn't it, lads?
**Warder 1** Brilliant
**Warder 2** A real laugh.

**Executioner** As soon as I turned up with the black hood on, the crowds would cheer——
**Warder 1** And clap——
**Warder 2** And give it all that.
**Executioner** Yeah, and it was good prospects, too. Remember, they used to say——
**Warder 1** "Be an executioner and get ahead".
**Executioner** Yeah. Of course, it wasn't always easy. To be honest, some of our customers didn't even want to be decapitated.
**Warder 2** We've had them running round the Tower yard, hopping over walls——
**Warder 1** Behind bushes——
**Warder 2** Yeah, giving it all that——
**Executioner** And muggins here has had to chase them waving this whopping big axe about.
**Warder 1** Tell them about the leather necks.
**Executioner** Oh, right, the leather necks!
**Warder 1** Some necks are so tough——
**Warder 2** The axe just bounces off.
**Warder 1** Yeah, he takes a big swipe and *doing!*
**Warder 2** Hardly a scratch.
**Warder 1** He's hacking and chopping away——
**Warder 2** Giving it all that——
**Executioner** Lads! Er, try and be a bit sensitive.
**Warder 1** Oh, yeah, sorry.
**Warder 2** Sorry about that.
**Executioner** Well, anyway, the point is: it was all a big game, then.
**Warder 2** Yeah, if the King didn't like you, then *chop!*
**Warder 1** Instant throat surgery.
**Warder 2** Take the weight off your shoulders and all that.
**Warder 1** And it was just hard luck, mate.
**Executioner** It was fine within reason, but now, it's different, isn't it?
**Warders** Yeah.
**Executioner** Take little Catherine just then. She looked me straight in the eyeball——
**Warder 1** She blessed him.
**Warder 2** That's right, she said "God bless you" and all that.
**Executioner** Shut up, you two! Anyway, one quick swipe—swish clonk, that was it.

**Warder 2** Bye-bye, little Catherine.
**Warder 1** She wasn't Queen long enough to have her picture painted.
**Executioner** And what for?
**Warder 1** Yeah, what for, really?
**All** Nothing!
**Executioner** Frankly, ladies and gentlemen, it's no fun any more.
**Warder 1** We know Henry's the King——
**Warder 2** And he used to be a big laugh and all that——
**Warder 1** But...

*They all look around*

**Executioner** (*whispering*) He has got beyond a joke.
**Warders** Right!
**Executioner** Well, thanks for listening, and as we say in the trade——
**All** Keep your scarves on!

*They exit*


SCENE 6

*... in which Henry finds he has to justify himself*

*Old Henry is lying feebly in bed. Catherine Parr, Thomas Cranmer and the Doctor are beside him*

**News-reader** Tudor News can already report that since Catherine died in the tower, her spirit has been seen to walk around the galleries of Hampton Court. Anyway, like Catherine, we too have about reached our end, and so we leave you now with one final report filed in January fifteen forty-seven.
**Henry** Who are you?
**Cranmer** Your Archbishop, Thomas Cranmer.
**Henry** I thought I executed all the Thomases.
**Cranmer** No, sire. Somehow I've survived.
**Catherine P** Makes you wonder, doesn't it?
**Henry** Who's she?
**Catherine P** Oh, Henry, not again! I keep telling you, I'm Catherine Parr, your sixth and last wife.

**Henry**  How do you know you're my last?

**Catherine P**  Because you are old, lame, fat, bald, and diseased.

**Henry**  Old? Lame? Fat, bald, and diseased? *Next!* I'll have you beheaded.

**Catherine P**  Stop showing off and drink your milk.

*The Doctor passes a goblet. Henry drinks feebly, then looks around*

**Henry**  Why is there an Archbishop and a doctor at my bedside?

**Catherine P**  Because you're nearly dead. Believe me, I know what dead husbands look like. I've already had two, you'll be number three.

**Henry**  My God, she's making a collection.

**Catherine P**  Look who's talking.

**Henry**  How dare you marry me when you've been married before?

**Catherine P**  Oh, come on, you're hardly fresh from the farm yourself.

**Henry**  (*struggling to his feet*) That does it. I'll chop you myself.

**Catherine P**  Here you are, then.

*Catherine passes Henry a big sword but when she lets go, Henry cannot hold it. He staggers sadly. Catherine gently leads him back to bed*

You have a rest first, then you can chop my head off. I'll wait for you.

**Henry**  How's the navy?

**Catherine P**  You've forgotten that too? Remember the French Armada a couple of years ago, you kicked six bells out of them.

**Henry**  The French? Pah! (*He spits feebly, then notices it's landed in his beard*) Very proud of my navy. My navy and my son Edward. At least I have a son.

*A mysterious bell slowly tolls continuously. Henry gets to his feet*

What noise is this?

*He looks around, but the others are still staring at the bed where he was lying*

The bell! Do you not hear?

**Doctor**  The King has passed on, my Lady.

**Catherine P**  He hasn't passed on.

**Henry**  See?

**Catherine P**  He's died. One day you might "pass on", but real men die.

**Cranmer** You wish me to give blessing?

**Catherine P** Might as well. Right now he's probably going to need all the help he can get.

**Cranmer** Lord, we beseech thee, welcome now the soul of our dearly departed Monarch and friend Henry...

**Henry** Stop this! *Stop it*, I say.

*The Lighting changes to an eerie state. Some spooky figures step on to the stage. We recognise Anne Boleyn, Wolsey, More, Catherine Howard, Cromwell, and others who were executed*

What morbid assembly is this? Begone!

*A terrible voice addresses him*

**Voice** Henry, prepare yourself to face the celestial council.

**Henry** (*shouting; defiantly*) What for? Who dares to summon me so?

**Voice** You are hereby called before the highest and most dreadful authority to answer the following charges.

**Henry** Charges?

**Voice** One, that you did endanger the souls of your subjects by repudiating the authority of the Pope.

**Henry** I had to have a legitimate son.

**Spooks** Guilty!

**Voice** Two, that in the course of your selfish pursuits you did unlawfully . execute many persons, including: Anne Boleyn, Sir Thomas More, Thomas Cromwell, Catherine Howard——

**Henry** Hah! Any other strong King would have done the same.

**Spooks** Guilty!

**Voice** Three, that you did authorise the destruction of many of the finest examples of English and Welsh heritage——

**Henry** But look what I built! Look at Hampton Court. Look at all the castles along the South coast.

**Spooks** Guilty!

**Voice** Four, you have bankrupted your country by waging costly and pointless wars with almost every other nation in Europe.

**Henry** I bet I won't be the last.

**Spooks** Guilty!

**Voice** Five, and finally, you did shamelessly neglect and mistreat both your daughters.

**Henry** Daughters? I had no use for daughters.

**Spooks** Guilty!

**Henry** You ungrateful little people! I have given England the greatest gift she could wish for. I have given you a Royal son to be your King.

**Voice** Henry the Eighth of England and Wales, may future generations be your judge.

**Henry** (*to the audience*) Let them judge me as they may,
my son will still be King this day
to that end I've lived my reign
and I would do it all again!

*Henry walks off proudly, ushered by the Spooks*

*The Lights come up as the very weedy ten year old Edward the Sixth appears on stage for his coronation ceremony*

*Everybody assembles round Edward the Sixth to sing the finale:*

### Song 18: The Coronation Finale

**All**  God rest the old King and God bless the new
Angels protect him in all he may do
Hear us oh Father and help him we pray
as he leads us all as he feeds us all
every part of the day.

God rest the old King and God bless the new
Angels protect him in all he may do
Guide him to victory and help him stay true
Hear the belfry ring and the choir sing
Alleluia to you
Amen.

*The cast bow, the audience applaud wildly*

*Final Reprise of other songs as required, finishing with:*

### Song 19: The Body Rock Encore

It's the same old story since time began
too much power went to just one man

Don't let the victims die in vain
Just make sure it never happens again.

Or your body's gonna rock
your head is gonna roll
tomorrow six o'clock
you're gonna take a little stroll
put your shoulders on the block
start praying for your soul 'cos
your body's gonna rock
your head is gonna roll...
and you can't do a thing because
that's the wish of the *King*...
*Oh yeah!*

CURTAIN

# FURNITURE AND PROPERTY LIST

Further dressing may be added at the director's discretion

## ACT I

### SCENE 1

*On stage:* **News-reader**'s desk
Chair

### SCENE 2

*Off stage:* Little truck. *On it:* axe, block (**Warders**)

*Personal:* **Executioner:** card

### SCENE 4

*Set:* Artist's tools

*Off stage:* Drawings (**Henry**)
Piece of paper (**Messenger**)

*Personal:* **Henry:** folded note

### SCENE 5

*On stage:* **Wolsey**'s desk. *On it:* books

### SCENE 6

*Set:* Plans
Jar. *In it:* leeches

*Off stage:*     Strangely shaped bone on a thread (**Joan**)
                 Bag, bloody saw, drill, horrible device (**Doctor**)

SCENE 7

*Off stage:*     Lute (**Anne Boleyn**)
                 Bible (**Scholar**)

SCENE 8

*Set:*           Needlework

SCENE 9

*Off stage:*     Form (**Pope**)

ACT II

SCENE 1

*Off stage:*     **Executioner**'s truck (**Warders**)
                 Axe (**Henry**)
                 Suitcase (**Cranmer**)
                 Archbishop's hat (**Will Sommers**)

SCENE 2

*Off stage:*     Axe (**Henry**)

*Personal:*      **More:** chains
                 **Cromwell:** death warrant

SCENE 3

*Off stage:*     Sheet (**Doctor**)

SCENE 4

*Off stage:*     Block, axe (**Executioner**)
                 Small portrait (**Cromwell**)

*Personal:*     **Anne of Cleves:** bag


Scene 5

*Off stage:*     Axe (**Executioner**)


Scene 6

*Set:*          Bed
                Goblet
                Sword

# LIGHTING PLOT

Special light settings and effects may be added to enhance the songs or add to the atmosphere as required

Property fittings required: nil
Various interior and exterior settings

ACT I, SCENE 1

*To open:* Overall general lighting

*No cues*


ACT I, SCENE 2

*To open:* Overall general lighting

*No cues*


ACT I, SCENE 3

*To open:* Overall general lighting

*No cues*


ACT I, SCENE 4

*To open:* Overall general lighting

*No cues*


ACT I, SCENE 5

*To open:* Overall general lighting

*No cues*

ACT I, SCENE 6

*To open:* Overall general lighting

*Cue* 1    **Henry**: "But that's a funny name for a boy..."                    (Page 23)
           *Black-out, then bring lights up when ready*


ACT I, SCENE 7

*To open:* Overall general lighting

*No cues*


ACT I, SCENE 8

*To open:* Overall general lighting

*No cues*


ACT I, SCENE 9

*To open:* Overall general lighting

*No cues*


ACT II, SCENE 1

*To open:* Overall general lighting

*No cues*


ACT II, SCENE 2

*To open:* Overall general lighting

*Cue* 2    They all exit                                                        (Page 50)
           *Dim lights to represent a dank prison cell*

ACT II, Scene 3

*To open:* Overall general lighting

*No cues*


ACT II, Scene 4

*To open:* Overall general lighting

*No cues*


ACT II, Scene 5

*To open:* Overall general lighting

*No cues*


ACT II, Scene 6

*To open:* Overall general lighting

*Cue* 3    **Henry**: "Stop this! *Stop it*, I say."              (Page 69)
           *Change lighting to an eerie state*

*Cue* 4    **Edward the Sixth** appears on stage              (Page 70)
           *Fade up lights*

MADE AND PRINTED IN GREAT BRITAIN BY
LATIMER TREND & COMPANY LTD PLYMOUTH
MADE IN ENGLAND

www.ingramcontent.com/pod-product-compliance
Lightning Source LLC
LaVergne TN
LVHW051752080426
835511LV00018B/3308

* 9 7 8 0 5 7 3 0 8 1 0 1 9 *